The Future of the 'C

The Future of the 'Classical'

by
Salvatore Settis

translated by Allan Cameron

polity

First published in Italian as *Futuro del 'classico'* by Salvatore Settis, ©
Giulio Einaudi editore s.p.a., Torino.

This English translation © Polity Press, 2006

Published with the financial assistance of the Italian Ministry of Foreign
Affairs

Polity Press
65 Bridge Street
Cambridge CB2 1UR, UK

Polity Press
350 Main Street
Malden, MA 02148, USA

ISBN–10: 0–7456–3598–9

ISBN–13: 978–07456–3598–9

ISBN–10: 0–7456–3599–7 (pb)

ISBN–13: 978–07456–3599–7 (pb)

A catalogue record for this book is available from the British Library.

Typeset in 11 on 13 pt Berling
by Carnegie Publishing Ltd, Lancaster
Printed and bound in India by Replika Press PVT Ltd

For further information on Polity, visit our website: www.polity.co.uk

Contents

Die Antike ist uns eigentlich nicht gegeben –
sie ist nicht vorhanden – , sondern sie soll von
uns erst hervorgebracht werden.

Antiquity has not come down to us by itself,
nor is it within easy reach; quite the contrary,
we have to know how to summon it up.

Novalis, *Werke, Tagebücher und Briefe Friedrich*
von Hardenbergs

1 The 'Classical' in the 'Global' Universe

In 1967 Arnaldo Momigliano gave a lecture on the study of ancient Greek and Roman history to a group of secondary-school students at Erice in Sicily. This lecture, which as far as I know was never published, started with the question: why study ancient history? According to Momigliano, there are two very different, indeed conflicting, ways of answering this question: one is to say that all human events in every place and every time merit study and attention; the other is to argue that traces of *our* past that appear in our culture, language, monuments, institutions and countryside (in Italy for example) are so imposing that they catch our interest and force us to study the past in order to understand an important part of ourselves. If we accept the first reply, it would be a matter of complete indifference to Italians whether they studied the history or art of ancient China or of ancient Rome; if we accept the second reply, the study of ancient China will have a special significance for the Chinese, as will the study of ancient Rome for Italians. Indeed, if a European wishes to understand himself, he must consider not just the ancient Romans, but also the ancient Greeks, the ancient Hebrews and the Christian culture of the early centuries, which are indelible and interconnected parts of his cultural roots. Some forty years later we also have to ask ourselves whether this argument is still valid. In an era dominated by talk of globalization, the Graeco-Roman past may no longer be more 'ours' than that of the Chinese. The cultural landscape may have changed so much that Momigliano's distinction has become obsolete, and we are now off in search of new horizons.

A superficial but widely used response is that the 'classical' past has an enduring contemporary relevance because it contains and distinguishes the common roots of Western civilization, provides the European Union with a shared identity and embodies important values that, together with the Judaeo-Christian tradition, unites European cultures with others that have a European background, from America to Australia. This response is not convincing: if this really were the case, how would we explain the continuous, inexorable decline of 'classical' culture in the educational systems and the general culture of all the countries that should, according to their politicians' declarations, be drawing on those perpetual and immutable values? We are thus faced with a paradox, whose significance we need to emphasize and interpret: at the same time that we know (or are willing to learn) less about Greek and Roman antiquity, our cultural landscape is becoming increasingly dominated by the image of 'classical' civilizations (particularly the Greek one) as the sole and unequivocal root of all Western civilization, and the depository of its highest and unfailing values (such as democracy). This image, which is highly effective precisely because it is taken for granted, is becoming ever more established while widely held cultural attitudes and educational curricula are distancing themselves from the 'classical', particularly in the West. Our knowledge of Greek and Latin is shrinking and we read those literatures less (even in translation), but we talk about the Greeks and Romans more – in an increasingly lifeless, standardized and atrophied form. The more intellectuals, philosophers and essayists voluntarily lose their desire and ability to check personally and critically the intricacy and original meaning of 'classical' texts, the more they persist in seeking out a vague and unrestrained inspiration from them. This nearly always takes the form of absurd florilegia –

arbitrarily selected quotations used to legitimize one's own argument.

This tendency to hide one's decision to ignore 'classical' civilizations behind a profusion of quotations is not our greatest affliction. More serious and insidious is another feature of this process we generally assume to be unstoppable: when we use 'classical' culture in a vague and uncultured manner, we tend to put that culture on an unreachable pedestal and deprive it of its historical context. This in turn projects it onto a universal plane and in practice turns it into the weapon used with a degree of concealment by Western civilization to claim its superiority over other civilizations. The demand for 'strong' local identities capable of competing with the much feared and ill-defined realities of globalization is one response to our anxieties over loss of identity and panic over homogenization and absorption into a global culture. 'Western civilization' is undoubtedly one of those strong identities (all the stronger because it is not strictly local, but rather transnational and quintessentially 'global'), and the risks inherent in appealing to it without specifying the sense it is being used in and its implications are all the greater in a period – like ours – of threatened and actual clashes between cultural traditions often presented as innately and fatally opposed to each other. Examples are the West and the East, or Christianity and Islam.

No less interesting is the fact that random and unconnected elements or fragments of the 'classical' tradition emerge unexpectedly from the heart of non-European cultures. I will give just two examples. Hayao Miyazaki, one of the greatest Japanese authors of *manga* and *anime* (comics and cartoons), portrays in *Nausicaa*, perhaps his most substantial and demanding work (consisting of seven volumes), a post-technological world in which humanity struggles to survive on the margins of a hostile and massively polluted environment and in the midst of tribal violence and encounters with monsters of its own making. A young, innocent and non-violent princess perfectly attuned to nature saves the world. Her name, which is also the title of the series, is taken from Homer: *Nausicaa*. The second example concerns the aftermath to the 9/11 attacks on New York and Washington. In his first comment the leader of the Taliban, Mullah Muhammad Omar, compared America to Polyphemus, 'a giant blinded by an enemy he is unable to name', by a Nobody. The arch-enemy of Western culture and iconophobe who destroyed the colossal Buddhas of Bamiyan appears before the world as a reader of the *Odyssey* and attributes the cunning of Ulysses to the perpetrators of those acts of terrorism.

These examples are deeply disconcerting for two reasons (in one case, painfully so). The first reason is that they come from unexpected sources, from outside Western civilization which is generally perceived as having its roots in the Greeks (*ab Homero principium*). The second is that the extraction of the names and ethos of Nausicaa, Polyphemus and Ulysses from a compact Homeric context, and their insertion in such different and distant ones, appears to imitate closely the implicit norm in so much post-modern cross-reference: the disintegration of all that is ancient into decontextualized fragments ready for recycling and entirely arbitrary montage. This is particularly true when such behaviour is gratuitous and does not imply the paradigms of 'classical' antiquity that for centuries have been handed down in the European tradition by depth of knowledge and scholarship.

But is this really the case? Does Homer really belong more to 'us' than to the Japanese or Muslims? We should perhaps be more surprised by how these distant quotations from the 'classical' world are so intense, appropriate and effective. Perhaps these examples – and the many others that could be added to them (see chapter 16) – now belong to a much broader global spectrum in which 'classical' antiquity must take its place next to all the other antiquities – whether Indian, Chinese or Mayan – all equally legitimate as equivalent reserves of names, anecdotes, stories, quotations and curiosities. Although each of these antiquities has its own little troop of specialists, none of them can truly become the shared heritage of a future civilization if that civilization is to be elementally technological and one in which the distant past will be substantially consigned to oblivion. Or it might be the case that the past will be reduced to a hazy and formless backcloth that fulfils some ornamental role (which amounts to the same thing).

These reflections are not only relevant to current events such as the planned reform of Italian secondary schools and the continuous retreat of Greek and Latin studies (even without such reforms), but also concern a much wider context that goes beyond Italy and our period. They raise the question of the nature of the 'classical' and they force us to reflect on whether or not it still has a role in the contemporary world. If it does not, then it will only survive as the private entertainment of meagre coteries of specialists working on the fringe. But there is an alternative. One that we must examine, and it involves rethinking the nature and function of the Western brand of the 'classical' from its very roots. We need to identify its distinctive characteristics, if there are any. We have to assess whether they are alive and still have some significance within a markedly multicultural environment such as ours.

It is not at all obvious how we should go about reconciling this dramatically changed context with a detailed historical knowledge of the 'classical'. The main problem is that such knowledge comes up against the obsessive and near exclusive concentration on the present, so characteristic of our times. This distracts us not only from the 'classical', but also from history in general, unless it is very recent. This concentration on the present can perhaps be explained by the eagerness to understand the enormous complexity of a 'global' world. It is an effort to know it as it is today. Thus historical events (even ones that occurred one or two centuries ago) appear to be of little interest, or are intermittently summoned up for the purposes of current affairs (for example American policy), which gives them an air of fragile contemporary relevance that comes with a shelf-life. The past blends into the present, is assimilated by the present because of the pragmatic use to which it is put, and forced into an oppressive and virtual concomitance with the present, not very different from the frequent *petitio principii* by which it is taken as self-evident that other cultures must share our values. In this way, we fail to acknowledge diversity (in space and/or time) or at the very least, we minimize it. A professor at Berkeley, Nezar Al Sayyad, argues that Europe is losing its historical memory and is no longer able to perceive itself as a product of history, but rather identifies its traditions exclusively with modernity and hence with values that have come to be considered indisputable (Al Sayyad and Castells, eds, 2003). But 'no change is possible, once the inspiration for change [knowledge of one's own past] has been repudiated' (Kevin Robins, quoted in ibid.). Within this new cultural horizon, the concept of history as an uninterrupted sequence of events is losing ground to the use of history as a mere repository of *exempla* to be put together principally to provide an overview. The role of the 'classical' is simply a feature of this much broader process, but it is a very representative one given its extraordinarily central position in European cultural history, and because anything that can be defined as 'classical' lends itself to sporadic use by many people (as an *exemplum*). However, the 'classical' could be delivered from this utilitarian approach, if we could revive and analyse its extraordinary complexity and singularity with the necessary thoroughness.

It needs to be made clear that the 'classical' often emerges and re-emerges not so much in the form of a rediscovery as in that of a rebirth or *return*, as though it were a phantom with its own will and personality, and capable of returning whenever it feels like it. This theme took on a peculiar form in twentieth-century literature – that of the return of the gods to the modern world. Two contrasting examples will suffice – both from the American continent. The gods return to earth in Ezra Pound's poem *The Return* (1912):

> See, they return; ah, see the tentative
> Movements, and the slow feet,
> The trouble in the pace and the uncertain
> Wavering!

> See, they return, one, and by one,
> With fear, as half-awakened;
> As if the snow could hesitate
> And murmur in the wind,
> and half turn back;
>
> . . .

In J. L. Borges' short story *Ragnarök* (1960), the gods unexpectedly rush into a lecture hall at Buenos Aires University to the tears and applause of everyone present. But it soon becomes clear that

> centuries of their savage life on the run had atrophied all that was human in them; the crescent of Islam and the cross of Rome had been unforgiving with these refugees. Low foreheads, yellow teeth, scanty moustaches of mulattos or Chinamen, and brutish expressions revealed the degeneration of the Olympian race ... We suddenly understood that they were cunning, ignorant and cruel like ageing predators; ... we took out our revolvers and joyfully put the gods to death.

It would be difficult to think of two more different images of this feared and longed-for return. Pound's gods are unsullied figures from Olympus who have just awoken from a prolonged sleep (Yeats claimed, 'these lines seem the translation of some unknown classical Greek poem'), whereas Borges' gods are unrecognizable half-castes and therefore have to be killed.

Perhaps Yeats was wrong: no ancient poet would have ever written Pound's words. Perhaps the gods of the ancients were never icy and immaculate like snow. Perhaps the Olympians were quite the opposite and never refused (never stopped) mixing with human beings, and not just in Greece. Apollo resided in Delos and Delphi, but every now and then he flew to the far north to live amongst the Hyperboreans. Dionysus wandered through Egypt, Syria, Thracia, Arabia, Persia and India. Aphrodite was not born in Cyprus but she stayed there during her long journey from the East to the West. Zeus himself visited the Ethiopians, and he would never have become the lord of Olympus if Amalthaea had not nursed him and the Curetes from Phrygia protected him in a Cretan cave. Some other gods migrated along the silk route and reappeared centuries later in Japanese art. They had been transfigured but are recognizable in the context of another polytheism (they were Hermes, Boreas, Heracles and Tyche). Like Borges' gods in Buenos Aires, the Olympians always mixed with other peoples and cultures: if we hesitate to acknowledge them in guises that seem impure, it is because we have created an unblemished image for our own purposes – an image that shines like marble or snow but is not necessarily true. Instead of seeking out the 'classical' on the snowy and inaccessible heights of Olympus, we should perhaps be looking for it on earth and using history to give it a name and some substance.

In spite of the tried and tested uses of the 'classical', its two halves – the Greek and the Roman – were very different. Roman history by its very nature aspired to become universal (as an extension of its empire that stretched from Scotland to the Red Sea and from Portugal to the Danube). It was the history of a 'known world' which even comprehended some vague notions of India and China, and was only ignorant of the 'new' continents to be discovered much later. It is also true that the Roman Empire was the model not only for Byzantium, which was its legitimate successor up until 1453 (and always called itself 'Roman' and never 'Byzantine'), but also for the empires of Charlemagne, Frederick II, Charles V, the Holy Roman Emperors until Napoleon, and finally Napoleon himself. In the East, the 'post-Byzantine' empire of the tsars used that title because, like the German kaisers, it perpetuated the name of the Caesars and the memory of their empire. Rome has become synonymous with the Catholic Church and its conspicuous universal mission precisely because it was the capital of the empire during the period in which the new religion was being founded. Hence the persistent ecumenical drive (in the actual rather than the figurative sense: *oikoumene* is in fact the Greek for all the inhabited lands). Yet claims for the universality and eternal validity of the 'classical' have for several generations derived from little Greece, one of the many Roman provinces and one that before Rome was torn apart by internecine conflicts between its hundreds of city-states. Greece had found short-lived unity under the Macedonian kings but at the price of losing the freedom of its *poleis*. These rulers pushed the borders of the Greek world as far as the Nile and the Indus, and in effect united the culture of the eastern Mediterranean.

Greek and Latin were the two languages of the Roman Empire, and later of the two empires, one of the east and one of the west, creating a fracture that survives in the separation between the western and orthodox churches. However, the cultural pre-eminence of Greece, as the cradle of 'classical' and therefore Western values and ideas, is the thread that runs through European history of recent centuries, as though the immense structure of the *Roman* Empire (which embraced the whole of modern Europe, North Africa and some regions in Asia) has been kept alive in our cultural memory by a sustenance that is mainly *Greek*. In spite of their immense and merciless power, Romans occasionally appear on the fading backdrop of cultural memory as simply the intermediaries of Greek culture or 'second-class' Greeks. Even such countries as Germany and England (i.e. cultural areas where no one knew anything about the Greeks during the 'classical' era) can look to the Greeks and not the Romans as their elected roots.

John Stuart Mill was able to write in 1859, 'The Battle of Marathon, *even as an event in English history*, is more important than the Battle of Hastings. If the issue of that day had been different (if the Greeks had not won), the Britons and Saxons might still be wandering in the woods.' This and a hundred other examples, which could be produced all too easily, suggest that the common roots of Western civilization across the barriers of peoples and times are to be found in Greek 'classical' civilization. In other words, the myth of an original and shared 'classical' civilization translates into a concept of Greek history as universal history, or rather as the essential key to understanding the modern world starting with its consequences *for us* (or what we believe them to be). Yet this image of Greek history as universal history requires the Romans not just as cultural intermediaries but as the institutional, military and administrative structure by which the Roman Empire created the right context for 'classical' culture to put down roots and spread geographically and over time. We can now see two different and complementary images of our debt to 'classicism', always supposing such a thing exists: in the first, it is principally Roman (as a result of the expansion of the empire, the cultural unification that this brought about and the values that made this entire process possible), while still including significant Greek elements; in the second, the 'classical' coincides with Greek civilization at its height, and the Romans were simply its first heirs and disseminators in accordance with Horace's oft repeated motto, *Graecia capta ferum victorem cepit, et artes intulit agresti Latio* ['Conquered Greece conquered its savage victor, and introduced the arts into rustic Latium'].

These disputes over the relative weight of the Greeks and the Romans in the formation of Western values (a subject we shall return to) do not touch upon the real problem, because they take as a given the centrality of 'classical' roots, their ability to found values, and their status as a 'universal history'. Although thoroughly tested by time, this grandiose image is now showing many deep fissures, however attractive it may continue to be. Let's examine one of them. In the example from Mill, the founding nature of 'classical' civilization is symbolized by the Battle of Marathon and therefore identified with a Greek victory (for Greek read European) over the Persians, who here represent an indeterminate and static Orient, the 'other' who is unchanging compared with the European who is characterized from the time of the Greeks by extreme dynamism and continuous progress. *That is why* it is the root and mother of a modernity that is wholly ours. There is a widespread belief that the Greeks sowed the seed that would blossom much later into events and values that today we identify with. This was the opinion of Hannah Arendt, who argued that neither the American nor the

French Revolution could have occurred without the example provided by 'classical' antiquity.

The contrast between East and West is almost always concealed or even denied in ideas and reflections like these, but nevertheless continues to exert its influence in an intangible and subterranean manner. Yet this approach, which once appeared to ensure a permanent place for 'classical' culture and guarantee its continued vitality in the modern world – almost as though it could be spread not only by Roman legions as in the past but also today by the arms, goods and technology of the West – has now come to sound like its funeral lament. What place is there for the ancients in a world increasingly characterized by the blending of peoples and cultures, the condemnation of imperialism, the end of ideologies, and the bold assertion of local traditions and ethnic and national identities in the face of all forms of cultural hegemony? Why seek out common roots, if everyone is intent on distinguishing their own from those of their neighbour? How can we boast of having defeated the 'others' at Marathon without remembering Algeria or Vietnam? How could we be so presumptuous as to demand that the Chinese and the Indians identify with the Greeks and Romans – thus implying their identity with 'us' who are wholly European – if we do not offer in exchange our own desire to identify with *their* antiquity? If our perception of the ancients and their role in a 'universal history' really is one that reduces universal history to the history of Europe and its expansion, then the ancients are (or risk becoming) the prototype for a doomed culture – for dead white men whose traditions will need to be killed off.

We therefore need to clarify the distinction between the values of 'classical' antiquity as developed by the Greeks and Romans, and the way they have been used in the last few generations to legitimize the West's hegemony over the rest of the world. But we also have to bear in mind how difficult it is to understand this distinction, particularly for those who feel offended or injured by the West's hegemony. It is not at all clear how much the decline of 'classical' culture can be associated with the development of a post-colonial cultural landscape. What is clear, however, is that the spread of super-ficial and persistent 'classical' references (particularly apparent in advertising and the cinema) is not preventing the expulsion of classical culture from our shared cultural hori-zon. Quite the opposite, it is accentuating and accelerating it. Indeed it is legitimizing the phenomenon, because it tends to conceal it. The extreme marginalization of 'classical' studies in our education systems and our culture at large is a pro-found cultural shift that would be hard to ignore, and yet we often do precisely that. Those who are most guilty of ignoring (or preferring not to notice) this cultural shift are those engaged in the painstaking study of classical disciplines; it is almost as if they take the continued existence and central importance of such disciplines for granted. This recalls Goethe's famous pronouncement that disciplines can self-destruct in two ways: either because they linger on the surface of things, or because of the excessive depth to which they carry their examinations. Both these things are happen-ing in the current divorce between the 'science of antiquity' and the use of antiquity in contemporary culture. Even though they use the same basic materials, contemporary cul-ture and the science of antiquity are travelling at entirely different speeds (and this is becoming increasingly evident). The first perpetuates and shows a particular fondness for a melodious, faultless and unchallengeable image of 'classi-cism', whereas the second, at least in its most advanced manifestations, has chosen to examine its contradictions, variety and flaws, and uses comparative studies and historical anthropology to discover the multiplicity of cultures that coexisted within the 'classical' world, their reciprocal influ-ences and relations, their exchanges with Eastern cultures, and the unexpected wealth of currents (in art, science and thought) that were then losing out but contained potential and embryonic ideas we need to rediscover. The 'Greek mira-cle' is thus turning into the *Grecs sans miracle* prophesied by Louis Gernet, and the ancient history and culture of the Greeks and Romans is becoming increasingly bound up with other histories and other cultures. The question remains, however, as to whether we will be able to refer to the eventual outcome of this new scholarly approach as the 'classical'.

3 'Classicism' and the 'Classical': Retracing our Steps

Such a complex and entangled approach makes the study of the Graeco-Roman world interesting, but it is not without its problems. It challenges not only the flat and uniform version of the 'classical' with its typically third-hand quotations, but also some of the major currents in the most prestigious and well-established traditions of 'classical' studies. Because of this it attracts concerns and protests, as well as plaudits. The real question, then, is what is the 'classical'? Which is the 'classical' that merits this name – the uniform and unchallengeable 'classicism' or the multiform and changing one? Perhaps both. This gives rise to further questions: how was the concept of classicism itself born, how did it develop and how has it been modified? How has the relative importance of Greeks and Romans shifted over the centuries? Do these terms have any meaning in the multicultural and 'global' contexts in which we move today and will continue to move in the future? Is ours the only civilization with roots in the Greek and Roman 'classical' world? Do we need to distinguish between a 'classical' for specialists and a no-nonsense 'classical' for everyone else? What is the relationship between the 'classical' and 'classicism' by which we mean a conscious backward glance towards the 'classical'? Is it true that the 'classical' and 'classicism' are typically Western concepts, or do we find equivalents and parallels in other cultures? We are therefore posing, albeit in a slightly different way, the question posed by Arnaldo Momigliano, which we took as our starting point: is the Graeco-Roman heritage really (or still) more 'ours' than the ones provided by the Japanese, Chinese and Indian civilizations?

In European cultural history, this problem takes on a special significance precisely because the idea of the 'classical' runs right through it like a kind of recurring obsession. In other words, European cultural history reflects its repeated waves of 'classicism'. We can start by saying that the 'classical' is a concept that is inherently *static* in that it designates an historical period that is by definition over, but it cannot have any sense and cannot become functional without the *dynamism* of nostalgia or repetition – without that driving force that in one moment pushes towards a return to the 'classical' and in the next pushes to outperform or go beyond it. In other words, 'classical' and 'classicism' act as a pair of concepts that give meaning to each other and legitimize each other. In other great civilizations such as the Chinese and Indian ones, there are well-known cults of the ancient (*gu* in Chinese) in the sense of the canon (*gu-dian* in Chinese), but there does not appear to be any equivalent of the range of meanings and values associated with the 'classical' in the European tradition, particularly the idea of the cyclical return which, as we shall see, seems to be peculiar to our tradition. There is an urgent need to carry out a comparative study of the meanings of 'classical' (or of related concepts such as 'canon' in some cases) in these and other traditional cultures – as far as I know, a need that has yet to be satisfied. Given the gaps in my knowledge, this study will fall short of that threshold which I hope others will soon cross, and I will attempt to develop arguments on the 'classical' and 'classicism' in the cultural context of what we call the West. However, I will point out that specialists in three great civilizations (India, China and Japan) have assured me that the terms used today to designate the 'classical' periods in the respective languages and cultures are in fact based on those used in European languages and were not developed independently.

Graeco-Roman antiquity not only gave rise to the socio-cultural mechanisms of what we call the 'classical' and what we call 'classicism', but also to the word *classicus* itself, even though it was only much later that this term came to designate the former two. However, we use 'classical' with reference to many other contexts and cultural realities: there are the classics of German or Italian literature and of the cinema, there is the classical era of the Mayan culture, and there is classical music. For Macintosh users, 'Classic' currently means the computer 'environment' that makes it possible to access out-of-date programmes; in other words it is a synonym of 'obsolete'. All these and any other wider uses of the term are outside the scope of this study, although they are in fact part of this term's success story. I will outline and retrace through history the term's application to the figurative arts – and will do so in a highly selective manner – in the hope that this will be sufficiently representative of a much wider cultural development.

I will start with some contemporary experiences and then go back over time to end up with a working hypothesis. This approach involves a few premises that also restrict the field of study. Firstly, the terms 'classical' and 'classicism' are quite distinct and almost opposites when they refer to Graeco-Roman antiquity, although they are also more or less interchangeable when applied to other contexts of cultural history (typically the France of Louis XIV). In the Graeco-Roman context, the 'classical' *comes first* and designates that which is original and paradigmatic, and that to which the various waves of 'classicisms' would *later* refer as the centuries passed by. In the words of Paul Valéry, 'The essence of classicism is the coming later. The order presupposes a degree of disorder that it is about to sort out' (*Variétés*, 1944).

It should however be understood that the use of the term 'classical' with reference to Graeco-Roman antiquity is by no means unambiguous, even if we restrict ourselves to one country and current usage. One example, this time American, will again suffice: the following note appeared in a brochure for an exhibition of Greek bronzes, held at the

Cleveland Museum of Art in 1989: 'The term *classical* is used broadly to describe the Greek, Etruscan and Roman cultures from about 1200 B.C. to A.D. 476, while *Classical* refers strictly to Greece from 490 to 320 B.C.' This didactic statement very clearly demonstrates that 'classical' can be used in a broad and a narrow sense (the highpoint of the classical period), the latter being highlighted, at least in this English-language case, by the presence of an initial capital letter. The restriction in meaning applies to both the temporal and the spatial (one and a half centuries as against seventeen, and Greece alone as against the entire Mediterranean and beyond). As we shall see, 'classical' does not only have a narrow and a broad sense; its meanings, even in relation to 'classical' antiquity, are many more than two. Given that the various uses of the term were themselves products of the historical process we will be retracing, the appropriate place for a brief terminological analysis is much further on in this book (chapter 11). One last point needs to be borne in mind: this subject defies all systematic treatment, precisely because it runs throughout European cultural history and has for so long enjoyed such a privileged position within it. I have therefore adopted a fairly eclectic approach and have exercised considerable licence in my choice of representative situations and examples.

4   The 'Classical' as the Dividing Line between Post-modern and Modern

The inclusion of isolated and defining elements of 'classical' or neoclassical origin is an essential part of post-modern aesthetics, particularly in architecture. The Donnelley Building in Chicago (1992) is a fifty-storey skyscraper for office use, the work of the architect Ricardo Bofill who has defined his style as *modern classicism*. All four external walls are crowned by pediments in the style of ancient temples and are full of similar references. As in other buildings by post-modern architects, the persistent recurrence of marble, columns, volutes and other supposedly Graeco-Roman elements does not at all imply a return to the 'classical' following the era of modernism, or indeed some hierarchy of values which gives pride of place to those things that are acknowledged to be 'classical' and can be used as such. On the contrary, post-modern projects refer to an extremely simplified historical model founded on the binary opposition between the modern and everything that preceded it (perceived as a monolith). 'Classical' in this sense essentially means pre-modern, and post-modern its recovery in a highly constricted linear timeframe that is declared with minimalist eloquence by the 'post' that *precedes* 'modern'. This sequence can be interpreted in two very different ways. Some believe that the post-modern has a powerful creative potential triggered by the death of modernity, and precisely because modernity is now behind it, the post-modern makes use of the ancient to construct a new language of its own – one that is complete in itself and comprehensive. For others, and I am more of this opinion, these post-modern experiments are little more than a self-referential penchant for quotations out of context, and this leads to a denotative and eclectic grafting of powerful, often classical or neoclassical referential elements onto the fabric of modernist rationalism. The persistent repetition of these quotations does not however succeed in hiding the degree to which they are at variance with the background fabric onto which they have been grafted. Still less does it invent a new one. Moreover the frequent adoption of an ironic and demystifying register that negates 'classical' vocabulary at the same time that it uses it (by decapitating or emptying columns, inverting the positions and roles of bases and capitals, and similar devices) does not demonstrate complete mastery of the expressive possibilities of this language, but rather the ability to repaginate it in a jokey manner, almost as if it were not an historical heritage but a virtual reality. Nevertheless, the 'classical' quotations in their various registers appear to fulfil the role of clearly distinguishing post-modern idiom from the modernist one, as is the case with post-modern architecture more generally.

If there really is something to 'learn from Las Vegas' (to use the title of the well-known book by Robert Venturi, Denise Scott Brown and Steven Izenour), it is the coexistence of and indeed equivalence between idioms and styles in the post-modern landscape, and among these idioms and styles the 'classical' in its various forms is simply one of many. Moreover the 'classical' of the Ancients is confused with its many revivals (such as the Renaissance and the Neoclassical). The miscellaneous ancient and Renaissance statues in Nigel Coates's Café Bongo in Tokyo, which are lined up on pedestals high up in a kind of inaccessible women's gallery that dominates the bar, are only there to evoke the nude statue as something exotic in a decorative or conventional manner, and it is of no importance what they represent or why. In this sense, the derivations of the 'classical' in post-modern architecture do not constitute a 'return to order', and do not stimulate reflections on the historical depth of this tradition. They exalt intrinsically fragmentary and incoherent classical references, and divide the ancient up into minimal decontextualized units that can be recycled arbitrarily (such as Doric columns made of white concrete by a company in Hamburg and sold in segments in order to create portals and porticos of variable height).

Post-modern architecture is not therefore a new season of classicism, but rather the symptom of the end of a tradition, and it seals the destruction of the paradigmatic status of 'classical' antiquity which for centuries had ensured that the European tradition continued to study and familiarize itself with the 'classical'. Even the repetitive nature of post-modern quotations, which only take elementary details from 'classical' art and are immediately recognizable at some ill-defined level of popular culture, cannot be seen as the metaphoric appropriation of the ancient to popularize it through its re-use in mass-produced and therefore democratized architecture. On the contrary, the 'classical' does not figure in the post-modern as a challenge to the present (or the future) by means of the past, and the post-modern does not popularize the 'classical'; it simply trivializes it. The reduction of the 'classical' ornamental lexicon to a few arid elements – always the same ones – impoverishes the 'classical' idiom, and it does so not because it wants to distil the kernel or essence of this idiom, but because it does not want to go past the surface of things; it is happy with very little.

And yet it is difficult not to wonder why post-modern idioms have annexed the 'classical' to their own territory and even used it to distinguish themselves from modernism, on the assumption that modernism had completely repudiated the 'classical' inheritance from former generations and the post-modern could therefore mark a return to it. This claim, although often implicit and not necessarily a conscious policy, raises the question of whether the divorce between modernism and the 'classical' really was so radical, and whether the post-modern can be considered a return to the 'classical'.

5 The 'Classical' amongst the 'Historical' Styles and the Victory of the Doric

The 'modern movement' (particularly in architecture) is only one of the many artistic trends of the twentieth century. The label 'modern' has been applied to this movement and many other tendencies and schools, but the frequency with which it has been used to define not just art but also literature, philosophy and science probably reflects our undying and unfulfilled desire for self-definition, and has little to do with any clear and unambiguous concept. What is clear is that the 'modern movement' in the first decades of the twentieth century tended towards a lack of decoration and promoted simple, strictly functional forms that reflected concerns over the proportions of spaces, and buildings whose surfaces were structured in accordance with clear geometries. It also repudiated the 'historical' styles used by the immediately preceding generations for their own ornamental and expressive vocabulary. The new freedom in shaping 'pure' three-dimensional form (generally without ornamentation) gave this movement an extraordinary experimental energy and also a kind of transnational unity which, in spite of the absence of a manifesto or single leading figure, soon transformed it into an international style, indeed *the* international style during the decisive interwar years. Two famous formulas wonderfully condense this crucial aspect of the modernist aesthetic: *Ornament und Verbrechen* ('Ornament and Crime'), the title of a lecture given by Adolf Loos in Vienna (1910), and Ludwig Mies van der Rohe's saying, 'Less is more'. Both express in terms that are both aesthetic and ethico-political their strong preference for an architecture based on the essential and the functional, as against ornamental embellishments. Both formulas convey the idea that decoration is not only an obstacle to an architect's creativity and ability to respond to the needs of a new society, but also mere passive deference to a tradition that had become tired and lifeless.

Conversely, the season of historicism starting as early as the 1830s staked everything on an artistic vocabulary steeped in historical knowledge which by that time the history of art, a newly constituted academic discipline, was studying and restoring. This artistic vocabulary was therefore attentive to the various idioms that stratified the European tradition and also prepared to bring about artificial revivals (Byzantine, Gothic, Renaissance, Baroque) after careful assessment of the functions required by new state and social structures on each occasion (civil-service buildings, theatres, factories, museums, and residential areas). They were occasionally joined by exotic variants, from the neo-Assyrian to *japonisme*. Purity of idiom then meant choosing between 'historical' styles, one that was considered appropriate to the occasion and the expression of a function, a national identity or a tradition, whereas the opposite option, eclecticism, is characterized by free and lavish juxtaposition of semantic fragments taken not from one but many historical styles. The Ring in Vienna, with its *eclectic* mixture of buildings each in its *own individual* historical style, is a perfect example of a balance between the two tendencies: each building refers to an historical period whose style it has adopted, while the whole celebrates the plurality of styles as diversity and as an historical sequence. The stratification of historical styles on display there in a synchronic and sequential manner implies a vision (or an authority) capable of analysing the course of history and exerting a kind of synoptic control, almost as if the royal and imperial city were putting itself forward as both summary and highpoint of European history.

It was in this cultural framework of extraordinary complexity that the heirs of the 'classical' found themselves competing with the idioms of other revivals, just as words of Greek or classical Latin origin compete in modern European languages with medieval Latin, Romance or Germanic terminologies. Are we obliged to infer that the 'classical' was now on a par with the neo-Baroque and the neo-Gothic in a panoply of possibilities all of equal value? A simple reflection would suggest rejecting this conclusion as superficial: many of these 'historical' styles, whose revival was shortlived, were in turn full of elements (both structural and ornamental ones) that had been consciously and intentionally derived from the 'classical'. Such elements varied from Corinthian leafage and friezes of palmettes to the poses of men, women and animals in history paintings. The historical styles were not inward-looking but referred back to the 'classical' in what might be called a secondary manner, but all the more effective and eloquent for that, particularly in the case of the Renaissance, whose essence the nineteenth century singled out and defined as the 'rebirth of (classical) antiquity'.

No less important was the way in which the parallel experimentation with different historical styles (including those markedly affected by 'classical' elements) played in a more fundamental and more hidden manner with the new technological possibilities that were transforming the architect's trade. Particularly significant was the use of reinforced concrete and metallic structures usually concealed behind stonework or brickwork, but more rarely displayed in full view. In other words, the re-use of a particular 'historical' style (on the exterior of a building) and the adoption of new building technologies (within the building's structure) had the effect of mutual legitimization: those groundbreaking fusions made it possible to be entirely contemporary in the representation of the Gothic or the Baroque. In other words, it was possible to put the technologies of the present at the service of history. This relationship between structure and surface enabled the 'classical' to experience a new season, albeit in a very particular variant, and in this it differed from every other historical style.

The 'modern movement' drew sustenance from the increasing antithesis between the essential geometries of the load-bearing structure and the ornamental superstructures that hide the physical and tectonic forces at work in buildings behind leafage, capitals and carved and painted architraves in accordance with historical styles. Thus it could be said that ornamentation is a crime, in that it obliterates the structure of buildings by covering them with a decorative skin that captures all the attention, and argued that 'less' ornament meant 'more' in terms of functionality, expression and the development of form – in other words, 'modernity'. In this way, all the historical styles (including the 'classical') tended to be dismissed as ornamentation, and consequently their possible re-use was rejected as an unacceptable anachronism. The 'classical' could not avoid being affected by this general condemnation. However, the new rationalism and cult of the essential sought models and precedents, and while the new technologies relegated historical styles to the status of point-less epidermis, there was still a need to find an authoritative and meaningful model somewhere in 'classical' antiquity. And it was found in the 'pure' expression of the Doric style.

The Doric style was interpreted not as one of the many ways in which 'classical' syntax could be adapted, but rather as the very essence of a primitive and uncorrupted Hellenism, in which structure and form come together at the highest level. One of the most dazzling examples is a project that was never realized. This unforgettable icon of modernism was the project submitted by Adolf Loos in the 1922 competition for the head office of the *Chicago Tribune*. The architect, who had dared in 1909–11 to build a bare six-storey building (now known as the Looshaus) in front of the Hofburg in Michaelerplatz in Vienna, proposed that Chicago should have a skyscraper in the form of a gigantic Doric column, which was to contain twenty-one floors of offices on top of the eleven floors in the enormous square base.

Entrance into the base was to be through a portal flanked by two Doric columns two storeys high. The office windows were to open in the flutes of the column. The Doric order was therefore interpreted not as ornament but as pure form, and therefore remarkably suited to modernity, especially if enlarged as though by a pantograph to a structure of dimensions that would have been unthinkable to the Greeks and only made possible by modern building technologies and the new aesthetics of skyscrapers.

The 'classical' provided a similar degree of legitimacy to a new art form, the cinema. At one point in *Cinematografo come strumento di liberazione e come arte di trasfigurazione* (written at about the same time as the famous Italian film *Cabiria*, which came out in 1914), Gabriele D'Annunzio likens the white screen, a symbol of modernity in many twentieth-century texts on cinema, to the 'naked wall of a sublime nakedness, which seems to have been made for the apparitions of tomorrow ... placed on the side of the Athenian Acropolis that dominates the theatre of Dionysus' (this text was pointed out to me by Antonio Costa). Cinema was perceived as a Dionysian art: the white of the screen was like the blinding splendour of marble struck by the Greek sun, and the new aesthetic of the (cinematographic) movement was centred on the marvellous and the metamorphic. Therefore 'in this text, using a language that appears to have been borrowed from the futurists and an iconoclastic tone directed against the "old" theatre, D'Annunzio ... does not quote Meliès but Ovid's *Metamorphoses*' (Costa again). P. A. Gariazzo echoed these reflections in 1919: 'Dionysus leads the phantasmagorical procession, shadows and yet more shadows amongst the shimmering haze.' For both the Italian poet and the Viennese architect, the 'classical' is seen as something unquestionably pure, bare and essential: a white page on which the moderns could experiment with the reclaimed freedom to write new words, new architectures and new experiences. This concept of the 'classical' as a *tabula rasa* did, it is true, mean the rejection of the paralysing mass of historical norms, but it also meant reaffirmation of the 'classical' as the necessary point of departure (nothing can be written without a blank page). This was the 'classical' reduced to its bare bones, and therefore capable of acting not as a constraint but as a catalyst.

The victory of the Doric in modern architecture, which Loos wished to proclaim with the impressive forcefulness of his Chicago skyscraper, was very much in tune with the development by the Perret brothers of their 'structural classicism' which laid bare reinforced-concrete structures. Theirs was a rationalistic reading of the Doric order popularized by Viollet-le-Duc. Le Corbusier then produced an even more radical interpretation of this line. While designing a landscape full of a new architecture following his peregrinations amongst the ruins of the Acropolis in Athens, he distanced himself disdainfully from Roman antiquity ('for sale to millionaires') and perceived the Doric style as a sign of supreme, elementary and timeless purity. What were the reasons for this? Doric temples emanated an 'impression of clean threaded steel, the engineering of plastic forms achieved in marble with the same rigour we have learnt to achieve in machines' (*Vers une architecture*, 1923). It was therefore possible to isolate within the 'classical' one of its highly specific manifestations, the Doric style, and choose it for its consonance with the modern and the 'mechanical' rigour of its forms. Steel saved marble. These two materials discovered in each other a new relationship based on a close affinity. *Natura non facit saltus* – it may be the case that nature cannot be easily circumvented, but history can: the rejection of the decorativeness of the 'historical' styles (including the 'classical') could co-exist with the exaltation of the Doric as the touchstone against which modernity had to be compared.

6　The 'Classical' is not 'Authentic'

The 'classical' element that was particularly praised within Graeco-Roman antiquity (namely the Doric) was not intended as an example or synthesis of the 'classical' but as its rival. This was not an isolated case in the cultural history of those years. In the same early decades of the twentieth century, other disciplinary and artistic experiments examined the whole of Graeco-Roman 'classical' antiquity with the intention of breaking it up and extracting this or that element on the basis of intuition, sentiment or affinity according to how it could be exploited as a parallel or inspiration for the present. Archaeological research and the literary experimentation of poets and artists moved forward in unison, and even an accurate and systematic study (although very desirable) would be unlikely to pinpoint where this process began. In fact the process was not primarily one of reciprocal influence but rather of shared taste, and it received its initial sustenance from contemporary artistic avant-gardes.

Throughout the nineteenth century, historians of ancient art (particularly in Germany) put together an eloquent 'archaeology of art' (*Archäologie der Kunst*). This method of historical reconstruction hoped to uncover the manner in which ancient art had developed by bringing together the study of literary sources and the analysis of monuments in an unprecedented effort to get closer to the lost originals of

Greek art. They started by examining copies from the Roman era, once they had been identified, along with readings of texts by Pliny, Lucian, Pausanias and other ancient writers to re-create an idea of ancient masterpieces lost forever, such as Polyclitus' *Doryphorus* and Myron's *Discobolos* (see chapter 12). Thus an unexpected role was found for the renowned corpus of 'Roman statues', which had gradually been collected in private and public galleries since the Renaissance and later in the plaster cast collections of artists, academies and museums, as well as in drawings, engravings and antiquarian books. The corpus was no longer required to witness the glory of Rome; it had become a document of Greek art. The same statues that had been considered worthy of emulation (and in this sense 'classical') at least since the fifteenth century, were now re-consecrated by archaeologists in university lecture halls and museums, and their destiny depended entirely on the sharp distinction between the 'Greek' and the 'Roman'. In his authoritative *Meisterwerke* (1893), Adolf Furtwängler extolled the philological method of archaeology (which he understood to be the history of ancient art), and used it to introduce newly discovered 'classical' masterpieces into his courageous rewriting of the history of ancient art for a public not exclusively made up of specialists. He put across his arguments through an original and extensive use of photography, showing that archaeological techniques could be fused with the methods of attribution Giovanni Morelli had developed in the history of art (as Bernard Berenson once remarked).

However this new 'connoisseurship' in the study of ancient art was soon to produce results of an entirely different nature: the numerous copies were devalued against the very few originals of Greek art that had been preserved or were now being uncovered through digs. The discovery of Olympia's pediments during the German excavations, which started in 1875, had already completely revolutionized the settled perception of Greek art. Further discoveries from Samos to Athens revealed more originals every year, ones that almost always had no reference in written sources and

for which there could be no attribution. Thus the history
of Greek art based on information provided by ancient
sources (particularly Pliny the Elder) and centred on artists'
names was being challenged by the parallel history of the
originals, the 'history of art without names' (*Kunstgeschichte
ohne Namen*), commencing with the anonymous masters of
the *kouroi* and *korai* which were piling up not only in the
museums of Athens but all around Europe. The idea starts to
prevail that the authentic nature of Greek art and the substance of its form could only be found in the originals, the
torsos that had been mutilated by the passing centuries. This
new aesthetic climate had a marked preference not only for
originals rather than copies, but also for 'genuine' Hellenism
rather than the peripheral one (the Hellenism of Sicily and
Magna Graecia). It also radically changed direction and
founded its difficult and rigorous option for the mutilated
but authentic torso on an historical and ethical rationale, thus
distancing itself from existing procedures for the critique of
copies.

Ernst Buschor, a German, was one of the leading figures
amongst archaeologists: his ostentatiously intuitive descriptions of works of art attempted to transform *ekphrasis* (art of
description) into 'object' itself, basing himself primarily on
contemporary poetry. In fact, his descriptions would be
unthinkable without Rainer Maria Rilke. Like Rilke, Buschor
perceived the primitive and already perfect youth of the
world in ancient Greek art, and believed that this should
be projected onto the present in place of what had been
the 'classical'. This search for a new, ideal state of grace in art
and civilization had a preference for the fragment over the
whole, which accorded with the exploration (starting with
Nietzsche) of fragments by Presocratics, who were attributed
at least the same significance as the corpus of Plato and
Aristotle. This cult of the fragment encouraged the writing
of aphorisms, all the more effective and penetrating for
their similarity to a torso and their need to be filled out
by the reader. The absolute value of the fragment became,
as Theodor Wiesengrund Adorno would write later, a

constituent element of 'modernity', and precisely because, as Paul Valéry would comment, the fragment contains an invincible need, the germ of something else, 'something that is worth more than a meaning: the obsessive drive to reach completion'. It is the peremptory eloquence of the incomplete. A fragment intensifies the senses, and sharpens the observer's sight. Or to put it very succinctly, it is 'modern'.

An unprecedented conflict was thus taking shape. On the one hand, the traditional image of 'classical' art was now firmly established by the corpus of the 'Roman statues', an idea of the 'classical' that perceived antiquity as a Graeco-Roman monolith codified by universities and art academies, translated into handbooks and collections of casts, and reflected and exalted in the display of museum collections. On the other hand, the new desire for authenticity was pushing for originals, particularly very ancient ones unknown to scholars and artists, having just re-emerged from 'uncontaminated' Greek earth to create a direct and unmediated link with it. As Ludwig Klages wrote in *Blätter für die Kunst* (a journal founded by Stefan George in 1892), there was a need to 'enter into the mindset of antiquity' and not simply to 'appropriate it'. However, this antiquity had to be carefully chosen and it was no longer the 'classical' in its former sense; it was the pure beauty of the ancient torso that leapt out of the earth where it had been waiting for centuries for eyes that could acknowledge its worth. It was this new and original Hellenism that sustained the culture and life of the present, and in particular the cultural formation of that generation and the one to follow. It was said that it could stir up a rebellion against the academic idea of the 'classical', as well as unheard-of thoughts on the present and the future. These tendencies followed close in the footsteps of Nietzsche with his predilection for the earliest period of Greek culture, and were founded on the 'authentic' rather than the 'classical' as it had been understood up to that moment.

This restored 'authenticity' undermined the roots of the supremacy of the 'classical' over the 'natural', which had already been disputed and was already outmoded. The 'authentic' could no longer be the supreme incarnation of the truth of nature and more 'natural' than nature itself (as the 'classical' had been); the 'authentic' was opposed to this, and moreover its secret affinities with the 'primitive' were being uncovered. Thus Christian Zervos, Picasso's friend and founder of the *Cahiers d'Art*, presented artists with a selection of images from Greek art in his book, *L'Art en Grèce*, in 1934 and for him Greek art was only that 'which can be found in Greece, as the main factor in Greek art is the natural landscape', because that art was entirely compatible with 'our generation's enthusiasm for the peoples' arts wrongly considered savage, and our profound enjoyment of primitive races close to nature'. Zervos asked his readers to become conscious of a 'taste for instinctive drives and measuredness and for bold invention and passionate involvement' in Greek art. He believed they would be able to do so 'because of the constant spiritual gymnastics that are forced on us by modern art', as this Greek taste was in 'the purest and incontrovertibly modern spirit'. In other words, the search for the 'authentic' led to the Greeks being associated with the 'primitives', but also suggested a move towards Cycladic and archaic art rather than the already faltering 'classical' canon.

Another approach sought out alternative routes within the 'classical'. The art of the western Greeks, it was increasingly argued, was distinct from the Greek art of Greece proper and Ionia because of 'a different plastic structure' (Langlotz, 1965) which possibly had been influenced by the culture of form amongst the Italic peoples with whom the Greeks had mixed in Magna Graecia and Sicily. The status of western Greek art was considerably modified as a result: while some, particularly north of the Alps, saw that art as peripheral in relation to the mastery of the principal current of Greek art, others, particularly in Italy, preferred to attribute it with an experimental nature, a consciously alternative approach to the problems of form, style and aesthetics. The most original of these scholars, Pirro Marconi, adopted the term 'anti-classical' to define this phenomenon, and others later came up with 'a-classical' and 'hetero-classical'.

Although Marconi appealed to the 'spontaneous' rather than the 'authentic', this typically Italian development also detracted from the 'classical', which 'does not encompass the entire world of expression' (Marconi, 1930). The 'anti-classical' became 'a movement reacting to the classical' for which it was possible to claim a certain modernist quality: in other words, it was a kind of ancient artistic avant-garde that could be made 'contemporary' once again and therefore put forward as a model for contemporary art (Etruscan art encountered a similar treatment during this period, once again in the name of its home-grown 'Italian' nature).

The 'classical' as it had been developed over the preceding centuries was no longer sufficient. In order to nurture the 'modern', it had to produce powerful antibodies from within. It had to generate alternative lines of creativity and suggestions for experimentation, and legitimize the primitive and the anti-classical as well, by embracing not only the centre but also the margins and even the deviations of ancient art. It had to come to terms with the ideas of the avant-garde.

7   Greek 'Classical' versus Roman 'Classical'

The division between the Doric order and every other 'classical' ornamentation, and the one between the knowledge accrued from Roman copies of Greek statues and the taste for authentic, newly discovered Greek antiquity were not the only examples of a profound rift between two irreconcilable parts of the Graeco-Roman 'classical'. An even more radical shift in viewpoint occurred around 1900 on the other front: Roman art. The new ideas were not the result of learned discussions between specialists; indeed, here again the protagonists had their eyes firmly fixed on contemporary art. According to the interpretative paradigm that had prevailed since Winckelmann, Roman art was the final sterile phase of Greek art, its senile decadence (see chapter 8). Franz Wickhoff and Alois Riegl challenged this vision and re-evaluated Roman art. Although they approached the question from different directions, their ideas converged and both chose to judge Roman art not in terms of what preceded it (Greek art) but of what followed it (medieval art). The idea of decadence was not only abandoned but transformed into a positive force that explained the success of medieval artists and their cultural background rooted in late Roman art. It became a collective *Kunstwollen* (artistic intention – a term coined by Riegl), which profoundly changed the way artists and their public perceived the world.

The distance of the Romans from the Greeks was not denied, but reinterpreted not as degeneration but as the creation of a consciously new language and taste. Indeed Wickhoff saw the demise of Greek naturalism as coinciding with the birth of the Roman illusionistic representation of reality. The contrast between naturalism and illusionism contained an inherent hierarchy and value judgement, given that Wickhoff considered his favourite artists, Velázquez and Rembrandt, to be illusionists (*Die Wiener Genesis*, 1895). This critique, as expressed in Riegl's *Spätrömische Kunstindustrie* (1901), strongly implied a connection with the artistic experiences of the French and Central European avant-garde. Riegl's entire system was in fact created to explain and reassess late Roman art as the one that expressed the third dimension through a pictorial representation of perspective proportionate to viewing from a distance. However, Riegl defined the Graeco-Classical period as *normalsichtig* (having normal vision) and the late Roman period as *fernsichtig* (presbyopic). He also believed that this Roman 'presbyopia' increased the power of observation and was a break with naturalism that made it possible to increase the expressive potential of art. With its perhaps overly normal viewpoint, the 'classical' had constituted an advance in relation to the *nahsichtig* (myopic) of Egyptian art, but this progress had its own limitations, given that the *fernsichtig* nature of late Roman gave rise to all the developments of European art from the Middle Ages to Rembrandt and then to the Impressionists. Such theories were not popular amongst archaeologists (Furtwängler thought them a troop of 'hussars charging' into the study of antiquity), but others found them more attractive and amongst these was Peter Behrens, who drew his architectural lexicon from Riegl (see Anderson 2000). These theories encouraged people to look on Roman art not as a lifeless copy of Greek art, but as something uniquely itself; it could even be regarded as the common European idiom from which medieval styles were to develop.

Could Roman art be considered 'classical', either before or after this Viennese development? For Winckelmann there was nothing that deserved the name of 'Roman art', and at the most you could talk of a 'Greek art under the Romans' or in other words, Greek art during its final decline. The idea of decadence in art, which was so central to understanding the regressive role of Roman art from Winckelmann onwards, was not at all new. However, it did not base itself on a distinction between Greeks and Romans during the Renaissance. The highly influential Giorgio Vasari, who wrote *Lives of the Artists* (1550, 2/1568), considered Roman art to be the pinnacle in the development of ancient art, as the style 'more divine than all the others', and contrasted it with the two variants of what we call the medieval: the Goths and the 'ungainly Greeks', by which he meant the Byzantines. All Graeco-Roman antiquity was seen as a whole, and the fall from that 'divine manner' as a sudden catastrophe rather than a slow historical process. When they rejected the interpretation of Roman art as decadence, Wickhoff and Riegl were certainly not attempting to resurrect that vision; any attempt they made to save Roman art was not based on its claim to be 'classical' but rather on its potential which was then actually developed in the Middle Ages. The two opposing evaluations of Roman art – 'decadence' or a new and independent *Kunstwollen* – share one important factor: they both contrast Roman art with Greek art, but accept that the former contained significant elements of the latter. Even the Viennese campaigns of Wickhoff and Riegl were unable to undermine the unchanging understanding that Roman art contained both 'Roman' elements (however they might be defined) and 'Greek' elements. This led to the widely held perception of Roman art as shifting between two opposing poles: on the one hand there was a *courtly* art which tended to adhere to the 'classical' canons, and on the other an art that diverged from them and would finally triumph in late antiquity and again in the Middle Ages. Bianchi Bandinelli (1967) called this divergent art 'plebeian'. Precisely because of this duality, which came to be emphasized in the twentieth century, Roman art is delicately balanced between the 'classical' and the non-'classical'.

In the eighteenth century, arguments over the 'classical' canon started to produce two opposing camps, one that considered it purely Greek and the other that claimed it for the Romans as well. The discovery of Doric temples in Agrigento and Paestum in the first half of the century revealed building norms that were incompatible with those of Vitruvius, which until then had been considered universal. In the meantime, the idea of the 'classical' being centred more on the Greek world than the Roman one was gaining currency first in France and England, and later in Germany. This inspired travels and the examination of Greek monuments, and planted the first seeds of a Greek revival in architecture. And of course, a few Greek sculptures ended up alongside Roman ones in aristocratic collections. The Marquis of Nointel explored Athens as early as 1674, and a few years later Jacob Spon's *Voyage* (1678) contained the first account of the Greek Doric style in print. In England more important advances were encouraged by the Society of Dilettanti (founded in 1732), which suggested extending the Grand Tour to Greece, rather than restricting it to Italy as in the past. One of the results was the journey of James Stuart and Nicholas Revett, who spent two years in Athens drawing the monuments and then published their celebrated *Antiquities of Athens* in 1762. As suggested by a contemporary motto, 'Greek taste and Roman spirit', antiquity was still perceived as a whole, but the taste (the 'classical') that the figurative arts had to measure up to was decidedly Greek. However, the crucial contribution to this new Graeco-centric vision of antiquity came from Germany – from Winckelmann's prodigious *Geschichte der Kunst des Alterthums* (1764), which raised Greek art to a paradigm for artists and for the education of elites. The rebirth of the Doric was then embodied very effectively by C. G. Langhans's Brandenburg Gate in Berlin (1788–91), which was based on the Athenian Acropolis. This was followed by F. Gilly's projects and the rich and consistent work of K. F. Schinkel. On occasions the latter chose to use brick and terracotta, for instance in the Bauakademie (with reliefs over the main entrance inspired by those of San Petronio in Bologna), but when it came to palaces and royal villas he opted decisively for the Greek Doric, considered the pinnacle of the architectural hierarchy. The plans he submitted in 1834 for the royal palace of King Otto (the Bavarian prince who became the first king of Greece) proposed building on the Acropolis and removing all the later buildings except for those of the Periclean age, which were to be part of the palace gardens.

The 'new' temples and buildings that emerged from oblivion in Paestum, Agrigento and Athens were soon set up as the alternative to Roman architecture which had dominated the field since the Renaissance. However, the Graeco-centric line was never able to oust the Roman line entirely. The English could not forget that the Greek Revival had been preceded and stimulated by the Palladians who could be traced back to the Romans through the works of Andrea Palladio. When the French carried out further digs at the Foro Romano, English architects rushed there to survey and record the area. Buildings in the Greek style, such as William Wilkins's Grange Park (1808) and B. H. Latrobe's Bank of Pennsylvania in Philadelphia (c.1800) alternated with ones in the Roman style, such as the Fitzwilliam Museum in Cambridge and the Town Hall in Birmingham. There were also attempts at compromise solutions: whereas the Walhalla, the shrine to the German nation desired by King Louis I of Bavaria, was created by Leo von Klenze as a Doric temple inspired by the Parthenon (1830–42), Karl von Fischer's initial plan (1809) was for a kind of Roman Pantheon with a Greek Doric portico. The two currents came together and crossed on more than one occasion. It is true that the marbles from the Parthenon now in London and the sculptures taken from the pediments of the Temple of Athena Aphaia at Aegina now in Munich marked the advent of museums that were more Greek than Roman, but their dates of acquisition (1802–6 for the Elgin marbles and 1812–13 for the Aeginetan sculptures) were in fact of the same period as the Musée Napoléon, which was principally Roman in character and in the tradition of the papal collections in Rome. Indeed the Musée Napoléon took the *Laocoön*, the *Apollo Belvedere* and a hundred other statues from those papal collections.

The Hellenophiles did come across some opposition even amongst aspiring and professional architects. Readers of Vitruvius and those who were familiar with the Pantheon might have been disarmed by the sight of a Greek temple, but equally they might have taken some convincing that it constituted a higher level of 'classicism'. The unknown Graeco-Doric order was clearly more ancient than Vitruvius, but was it more worthy of imitation (more 'classical') than the Romano-Doric or Tuscan ones? Piranesi thought not, and argued for the primacy and originality of Roman architecture. He believed in its autochthonous origins (Piranesi, ed. Wilton-Ely, 2002). They could not have been Greek, and were, if anything, Etruscan, a model on which even the Doric of Paestum was based (Paoli, 1784). Piranesi's belief that the 'classical' developed entirely within Italy and was dominated by Rome's values and traditions had deep roots in Italian antiquarianism. This also opened up the possibility of the 'classical' (or some of its specific interpretations) being used in the creation of a national culture. However Piranesi, who believed in the primary role of the Etruscans and Romans, was on the losing side and was destined to clash with the increasingly dominant taste for the Hellenic, as demonstrated by his fierce polemic against Mariette in 1765.

8   The 'Classical', Liberty and Revolution

The importance attached to the figurative arts in eighteenth-century society does not by itself explain the intensity of the debate that contrasted the 'Greek' and the 'Roman' at the time. There was much more at stake than a preference for either Pantheon or the Parthenon: there was in fact a clash between 'Roman' and 'Greek' ideals of morality and behaviour, which involved Europe's intellectuals, philosophers, academies and courts. There was also a search for new sources of ethical and pedagogic inspiration. Of course, some virtues that were considered typically Roman had encompassed essentially Greek concepts (particularly those of the Stoics), which had however become known through Latin sources before Greek ones. We might say that they were therefore dressed up in the Roman toga, almost as if the success of Roman arms vindicated Roman ethical goals (even those which were actually Greek). *Thus* vindicated, they were presumably easily recyclable.

For centuries it had appeared obvious that the legacy of the ancients had to be treasured, but Plutarch's popularity meant that the relationship between the Greeks and the Romans was often seen more as a moral parallel than as an historical sequence. In his *Parallel Lives*, Greeks and Romans march side by side, and much was made of their education, character, vices and virtues. A work written in Greek during the

Roman era became a thematic repertoire of virtues; these virtues belonged to the ancients, but were perceived through Roman eyes. According to this synoptic view, the sense of unity in the Graeco-Roman world prevailed over the differences and fractures that divided them. In the eighteenth century Socrates was seen as a model of civic virtue, but through Cato and therefore in a manner that was more Roman than Greek. If there was an alternative to Socrates-Cato, it was a Socrates-Christ, as Rousseau suggested in *Émile* (1762).

However, this unitary concept of antiquity was to explode and fragment during that century. Greeks and Romans were treated increasingly as competing models and not parallel ones. The ranks of the Hellenophiles swelled and chose to concentrate on the Greeks, while attributing a secondary and contrasting role to the Romans. This was the context in which Greek art took on a sudden prominence, in spite of being mainly known through sources rather than works of art themselves, and almost magically became the sparkling core of a vision that embraced not only form but also the world and life itself, and could therefore radiate its power and inspire contemporary values.

J. J. Winckelmann was the hero of this process. Antiquarians of the old school such as Comte de Caylus had already posed the problem of distinguishing Greek art from the Roman, but their ideas remained very vague. With unprecedented audacity, Winckelmann put forward a new historical narrative of ancient art entirely dominated by the Greeks (as the Roman sources made clear). It was based on both the eye's interpretative power and the evocativeness of the written word, but could not rely on new acquisitions, although Winckelmann always longed to travel in Greece and carry out digs there. The spirit of Athenian statues had to be re-created from within the corpus of Roman statues through a process of elimination. This highly original prophecy on Greek art, which conquered Europe within just a few years, had yet further ambitions. The 'essence of art' that Winckelmann was refining was no scholarly evocation of the 'classical', nor was it some dispassionate antiquarian exercise; it was inspired by a singularly powerful drive and vision, and almost took on the status of a manifesto for artistic practice in the future. Its examples suggested new directions which would lead to Neoclassicism. Greek art as evoked and envisaged by Winckelmann immediately acquired stature and became the basis for education not only of the artist but of cultured people in general, precisely because it was part of a vision permeated with contemporary values. The ethical ideal and the aesthetic ideal fused into one – into a vision that desperately wished to create not only a metaphysical understanding of Beauty but also a certainty that Greek art could generate a transformation of the innermost self of the educated. The beneficiaries of this enlightenment and intellectual discipline would be gifted with a richer and fuller inner life. The conflict between antiquity and nature, which had first arisen in the sixteenth century, was won by the 'classical', and the 'classical' absorbed the truth of nature and indeed elevated and fulfilled it, as had already been suggested by French art theoreticians (particularly Roger de Piles). Indeed, the Greeks embodied the perfection of 'natural beauty', according to Winckelmann, and had experienced nature in all its wholesome beauty, not only because of Greece's ideal climate but also because of its political regime which encouraged both a feeling for nature and a propensity for art.

This project presupposed that Greek art had such a central role within Greek civilization that it could be seen as representative of the development of civilization in its entirety, from literature to civic life. However, the development of art (reflecting a more general historical development) as described by Winckelmann did not present Greek civilization as a uniform landscape; on the contrary, he considered it a parabolic trajectory of four distinct periods, the 'archaic' style, the 'high' style, the 'elegant' style and lastly the 'imitative' style, which was followed by the final decadence. It was therefore possible not only to prefer the Greeks to the Romans, but also to identify the higher (more 'classical') eras within Greek civilization. His ethical-didactic project and his historical research became intimately interwoven in his eloquent prose, as he formulated a set of ideals that would become those of the burgeoning middle class throughout the following century. Even ideas that had been widely read about now took on an unexpected vigour. Thus, when Winckelmann claimed *edle Einfalt und stille Grösse* (noble simplicity and quiet greatness), he was in fact transcribing a *topos* that already existed in France, but the *noble simplicité* and the *grandeur sereine* of the Greeks celebrated by Fénelon, Du Bos, Mariette and the young Voltaire never had a comparable effect on their readers.

The centrality and efficacy of Winckelmann's treatment of an essentially political problem are even more striking: he extolled 'Greek liberty', the active freedom of the citizenry within the *polis*, which favoured the arts and sciences (*Pflegerin der Künste*). Liberty revealed the citizen's spirit to himself, gave him a joyful life and drove him to give the best of himself. This was why, he argued, liberty helped achieve the summit of artistic achievement, and once liberty came to an end (with the subjugation of Greece to the Macedonians and then the Romans), the arts started to decay. These thoughts concerned the future and not the past; they were not history but a prophecy, and therefore could be read (and indeed were read) in a wholly eighteenth-century manner as an attack on absolutism. Revolutionary France claimed the new liberties partly in Winckelmann's name. Speeches in the Convention and official documents, as well as books and pamphlets, declared that France had to become a new Greece. The empire of liberty had to become the empire of the arts (this doctrine provided the ideological justification for the massive transfer of sculptures from Rome to Paris, and the same shipment also brought Winckelmann's manuscripts). Once again, Winckelmann had not conjured up his ideas out of nothing: long before him, Temple Stanyan had argued the parallel between Greek liberty and modern liberty in his two-volume *Grecian History* (1707–39), which Diderot translated into French in 1743. However, the modern liberty that Stanyan compared with Greek liberty was the parliamentary liberty established in England following the Glorious Revolution of 1688–9, which removed James II from the throne and replaced him with William of Orange and his wife Mary Stuart. Stanyan's liberty was essentially the re-establishment of constitutional freedoms and the reformed religion. Thus the same historical parallel passed from one revolution to another with Winckelmann as its intermediary, but in so doing its impact and power of persuasion increased one hundredfold. After all, Stanyan's was a judgement on the recent past, but Winckelmann's a hope for the future. Greek liberty – essentially that of democratic and 'classical' Athens (Athens of the most sublime art) – opened the door to modern liberty. Only much later would Benjamin Constant (1819) understand that the modern idea of individual freedom as formulated by German philosophy and the American and French revolutions was very different from the liberty of the ancients, which concerned the right to participate in the state administration.

Winckelmann was not only promising the 'Greek liberty' of the citizenry running its own institutions, but also and above all the individual's intellectual liberty through aesthetic experience. A continuous thread ran from this moment through to Rilke's 'you must change your life' (*Du mußt dein Leben ändern*), but although Rilke would still seek the decisive factor for inner change in 'classical' antiquity, he would replace the *Apollo Belvedere* with a mutilated, anonymous but 'authentic' torso (Rilke, 1908). Equally, the visionary 'classicism' of Étienne-Louis Boullée and Nicolas Ledoux used reassorted 'classical' elements for a new vision of the world and the conquests of Reason. Boullée's unrealized plan for a cenotaph to commemorate Newton (1784), an enormous sphere to be surrounded by three lines of cypress trees on raised ground, was a celebration of experimental science. Boullée considered it fitting for the hero of the new cosmology to have a mausoleum that enlarged upon those of Augustus and Hadrian. This new, ostentatiously utopian and 'classical' lexicon would later appear to the likes of Max Dvořák as not only a parallel to the Revolution but also a precedent for the modernist rationalism of Loos, Perret and Le Corbusier.

9   The 'Classical' as a Repertoire

The neoclassical artists (who would not be known as such for one hundred years after the first of them started their art) now had an agenda for rejecting the Rococo and adopting the new style on a clear programme inspired by the Greeks, albeit through Roman sources, and also for a profound moral and political renewal of society through art. This programme fully accorded with the *idéologues'* reflections on art as 'moral technology' and a mechanism that penetrates the citizen's consciousness and generates new models of behaviour by appealing to sentiment and desire (and ultimately taste). Many people, including Diderot, thought that art's contribution to the betterment of society had to be placed along with science in a much wider framework. Art and science had to promote individual initiative and also direct the society as a whole. According to Louis de Jaucourt in the *Encyclopédie*, a work of art could thus be perceived as a pictorial machine designed so that the interaction between its different parts influences the observer morally. Its ability to draw the observer in emotionally was considered at least as valuable as an irrefutable logical reasoning. Diderot's *Salons* suggested, as far back as the 1760s and 1770s, that this was the direction in which thinking was going, and it was addressed primarily to the Third Estate rather than the old aristocracy. In place of Boucher's *fausse nature*, he put forward the *nature honnête*, which could now be identified with the 'classical' ideal.

Such ideas took on more conscious and systematic form after the Revolution and especially after the Thermidor (1794), and were taken up by such members of the Institut National des Sciences et des Arts as Cabanis, Levesque and David. In two *mémoires* of 1796, Pierre-Jean Cabanis argued that every individual perceives art as well as the world through *signes*, such as gestures, voice and physiognomy, then interprets them through past experiences and finally reacts with sudden feelings of *sympathie* that can be shared with society as a whole. From here it was only a short step to proposing, as he in fact did two years later, that in the interests of the Republic the *Institut* should encourage an art capable of *cultiver les citoyens* by controlling their emotions through a calculated aesthetic balancing act. It was not a matter of imposing a new morality from above, but rather using art to evoke inclinations within the inner self, which were believed to be inherent to human nature. Those inclinations were reason and the instinct for liberty. Indeed, nature, nothing less, was the purest source of the new republican values. This miraculous balance between rational freedom of the spirit and aesthetic emotion that only 'classical' art could ensure in the highest degree had a name which was also popularized by Winckelmann: *Grazia* (grace).

He also assimilated the language of Newton and Condillac in the most extraordinary fashion to describe the interaction between observers and works of art. For example, *sympathie* was compared with the force of gravity in an attempt to provide the planned moral technology of art with scientific rigour and a law of nature governed by cause and effect. During the same period, Pierre-Charles Levesque (also in a *mémoire* for the Institut, 1796) posed the aesthetic question of the best construction of images for 'speaking to the soul' of the observer in a more explicit manner: *force* and *caractère* were his key terms. A painting's composition had to be based on draftsmanship and form rather than colour, and had to be oriented towards a clear perception of each figure in a clearly defined space and a reciprocal and balanced relationship, 'in accordance with nature'. The gestures of the figures had to be natural if they were to be effective, and they had to be universal if they were to speak to people's souls. However, such a universal vocabulary of human postures and passions, Levesque inferred, could only be found in one place: ('classical') Greek art, a timeless model because it was produced by the uncorrupted culture of the Greeks who were thus free to use their instinct and intuition in complete harmony with nature. Levesque's *mémoire*, although entitled *Progrès successifs de la peinture chez les Grecs*, was in fact addressed to contemporary painters. Given that there was not a single Greek painting to be seen, he suggested that they turn to Greek art in general, and in particular engraved stones and painted vases (i.e. the two 'genres' in which linear drawing dominated, in harmony with contemporary taste).

The manner in which artists greeted these appeals was immediately demonstrated by the example of Jacques-Louis David. His friend the antiquarian Antoine Mongez (also in a *mémoire* for the Institut, 1796) had appealed for artists to collaborate closely with antiquarians from whom they could learn not only the essential information on ancient customs but also their rigour in the composition of images, which was comparable to the syntax of a Greek sentence. He went on to claim that Greek art was like hieroglyphic writing in which every gesture had a corresponding meaning that was immediately understandable (even to the illiterate) because it conformed with nature. David considered this method to be 'erudite and reliable', as he said later to Delécluze, and he applied it with unstinting consistency. For example, the central figure of Leonidas in *Leonidas at Thermopylae* (begun 1798; exhibited 1814) was faithfully taken from an engraved stone reproduced by Winckelmann in his *Monumenti antichi inediti* (1767), who interpreted it as 'Ajax meditates on the death of Achilles'. The assumption was that the 'classical' image was capable of immediately and powerfully communicating the idea of a warrior hero during a moment of reflection, even to someone who knew nothing about the engraved stone depicting Ajax or Winckelmann's comment on it. It was believed that it was not only possible but actually necessary to put forward 'classical' art as a veritable language of nature – a language that was effective, meaningful and capable of speaking directly to the souls of the new participants in history, the great mass of illiterates.

Clearly this generous and abstract project was destined to fail. This does not make the intellectual and civic passion of men like Cabanis, Levesque, Mongez and David any the less impressive: it at least demonstrates that, although the artistic language and syntax they sought may not have affected the illiterate, it did produce the desired reactions in the minds of artists, scholars and the middle classes. Moreover the idea of art as moral technology and Greek art as a universal language had firmly re-established the belief in ancient monuments as an unchanging and readily re-usable repertoire as never before. In other words, it was the 'classical'.

10   The Rebirth of Antiquity

This idea was not new. Artistic practice had always involved the use of a repertoire of themes and norms that were just as much part of an artist's workshop tools as his paintbrush and his chisel. Just like any other piece of equipment, they could be handed down and they could be renewed. That repertoire was primarily a mental construct and as such the shared inheritance of artists, patrons and the public who needed to recognize the saints and heroes, and the stories associated with them, but it also translated into drawings, whether copies or improvised sketches. This stock of standard formulas could remain relatively static for generations and then be struck by sudden upheavals and rapid renewal in order to respond to public expectations that triggered fierce competition between artists. In the European artistic tradition at least up to the advent of Neoclassicism, the most powerful mechanism triggering the dynamic renewal of the repertoire was the periodic return of interest in 'classical' art.

Even in the Middle Ages, when very few 'classical' monuments were to be seen, there was no shortage of periodic returns to ancient models. However it took many centuries for those ancient artworks first to become models amongst an avant-garde, then to spread from one workshop to another, and ultimately to establish themselves as the norm. Italian artists were the protagonists of this process, which is generally referred to as the Renaissance (rebirth), and it could hardly have been otherwise, given that they were surrounded by more examples of 'classical' art amongst their ancient ruins particularly in Rome, and that occasionally these ancient artworks were put on public display. Throughout the Middle Ages, Roman sarcophagi were re-used in churches for the burial of notables, but capitals, friezes, reliefs, columns and statues were also recycled. The vast ruins of Rome and the pieces collected from amongst them acted as a kind of potential repertoire which could be drawn upon sometimes centuries after a particular sarcophagus or statue had been displayed in a public place. This ample repository of ancient marbles started to grow substantially from the fifteenth century as a result of the increasingly assiduous search for sculptures dug out of the ground, the creation of collections of antiquities and, above all, the way in which a new sensitivity for ancient works was developing among artists. Painters, sculptors and architects worked feverishly among these new antiquities enlarging their personal repertoire. They chose a gesture here and a drapery there, and neatly filled their notebooks with drawings of ancient art. From this they created the elements of a figurative lexicon that was defined as *new* precisely because it fostered the *ancient*. Each artist chose elements from that potential repertoire and adopted certain features and arrangements as his own. These selections were primarily governed by the principle of functionality (of a facial expression or gesture in an ancient model) in relation to the new context onto which these 'classical' elements were to be grafted, but also implied the *auctoritas* of the ancient models. And every time they were used to great effect, this authority became even more imposing.

Thus expressive formulas were reborn centuries after they had ceased to be used. One example is the gesture of desperation with both arms thrown backwards forcefully, which Nicola Pisano (c.1265) took from the *Death of Meleager* on a Roman sarcophagus that had been re-used for a medieval burial in Florence. He used its figure of a weeping

mother for the *Massacre of the Innocents* on his pulpit in
Siena. The same gesture was then adopted by Giotto for the
grief-stricken St John in his *Deposition of Christ* in the Cap-
pella degli Scrovegni in Padua (*c.*1305), from where it
spread widely amongst the workshop repertoires after having been neglected for ten centuries. For his *Deposition*
(1507), Raphael similarly took two gestures from another
sarcophagus depicting Meleager, which had been used for a
sepulchre in a Roman church. He very effectively revived
the expressive power of Christ's lifeless arm abandoned to
the impotence of death, and Mary Magdalene's tender act of
compassion in holding Jesus' hand in her own hands. In
these and thousands of other cases, it appears that artists
became aware of the deficiencies of their own repertoires
and the efficacy of the ancient one. It also seems that the
dramatic increase of the expressive and thematic possibilities of art (with the addition of stories of heroes and
'classical' myths) was increasing the visual vocabulary of art.
But a particular formula, however foreign to the contemporary repertoire, was usually chosen as a 'classical' model
precisely because it was morphologically similar. Its meaning
and its expressive qualities were therefore recognizable, but
considered to belong to a higher or, in any case, more effective register. The avid and feverish search for a new
repertoire of figurative motifs in 'classical' art first took hold
in Italy and then in the rest of Europe, and was soon codified
in treatises (particularly Leon Battista Alberti's *De pictura*,
*c.*1435) and biographies of artists (particularly Vasari's
Lives). Thus the 'classical' repertoire became increasingly
used in general artistic practice.

By observing and comparing ancient sculptures, Renaissance artists noticed that different ancient statues and
Roman sarcophagi depicted the same stories and used the
same expressive gestures, and their professional affinity
immediately told them that the ancients too had had their
own repertoires. As they interpreted ancient art through
their own workshop experience, they could not fail to notice
the continuous repetition of the same figures and gestures or

the same characteristics (such as nudity) and scenes (such as battles and hunts). Rhetoric had already codified the repetition of standardized formulas (*topoi*) that guaranteed effective argumentation. Given the dominant and pervasive presence of rhetoric (also taken from 'classical' models) as a universal mode for verbal expression and effective expression, the serial nature of particular figures, themes and iconographical features appeared to be just more *topoi*, ready for recycling and capable of being filled with different contents as each occasion demanded. This compulsive stylistic exercise (drawing and theorizing based on the ancient) not only attributed contemporary value to 'classical' art by turning it into a potent artistic vocabulary, but also drew legitimacy from it because of the aura of *auctoritas* surrounding the ancients (itself the result of the long departed but never forgotten Roman Empire).

This modelling on the ancient repertoire was the means by which the current repertoire and indeed artistic style were profoundly transformed in the period from the thirteenth century to the sixteenth. Just as new words and new literary devices were discovered when a new 'classical' text emerged from some monastic library, so the sight of a sarcophagus in a church could suggest new 'members' – gestures, poses and themes – to be added to an artist's 'composition' (in accordance with rules laid down by L. B. Alberti). Long before the French codifications of the late eighteenth century, 'classical' art could thus be seen as a perpetual and universal lexicon of formulas and gestures, a repertoire of 'technical' know-how concerning the representation of nature, movement and perspective as well as human sentiments and passions. It referred to a humanity that was considered self-evidently unchanging throughout time and which 'classical' art had known how to express with unequalled intensity and perfection. The more an artist like Raphael was able to assimilate that language intimately and embody the nobility of the ancients by reinventing gestures and motives, the greater his claim to become 'classical' too. In this drive to create a new art, the imitation of nature held pride of place, but there was also a growing perception that the perfect imitation of nature was already contained in ancient statues, and therefore the 'classical' was equivalent to the 'natural' or even surpassed it. A strong sense of the body, expressed by the frequent representation of nudes (which had already been considered an obvious reference to the ancients during the Middle Ages), would from then on have an important role in every perception of the 'classical'. The 'ideal' nudity of the 'classical' tradition, whatever attempts were made to justify it then and since, was always problematic from a Christian point of view, and whereas it had once been considered 'pagan', it now came to be considered 'profane' or 'secular'. And yet it encountered few difficulties in entering the churches to represent Christ and the martyrs (especially St Sebastian) in saintly nudity which was supposed to induce pious thoughts, although in reality it differed little from the heroic and carnal nudity of the ancients. Indeed it provoked protests among Protestants and caused church leaders at the Council of Trent to invent subtle distinctions and vainly attempt to build barriers against it.

The label 'Renaissance' is now used to designate either every movement to resurrect ancient themes, motifs and forms, or more simply a periodization referring to the transition from the Middle Ages to the Modern Era, almost as though the term were an explanation rather than something to be explained. Although the idea that the arts were reborn with Giotto was a recurring theme from the time of Boccaccio (*c.*1350) through to L. B. Alberti, 'Renaissance' in the sense we attribute to it today was the invention of Michelet (1840) and Burckhardt (1860), who bolstered and enlarged upon a terminology used in France since the late eighteenth century in such works as J.-B. Séroux d'Agincourt's *Renouvellement de l'art* (*c.*1790, published in 1811) and Lenoir's *Siècle de la renaissance* (1802). The term had two immediate implications. On the one hand, it defined the European cultural history of the fifteenth and sixteenth centuries as the age of the *découverte du monde et découverte de l'homme*, and therefore referred to literature, science, and political and social development, as well as the figurative arts. On the other hand, the powerful metaphor of rebirth, which also contained a latent reference to the Resurrection and the inner *renovatio* preached by Christian spirituality, clearly referred back to the 'classical' world. Given that rebirth can only occur after death, the Renaissance was a rebirth of *Antiquity*. For example, Filippo Villani (*c*.1400) was convinced that Giotto had restored painting to the position of esteem and renown that it had enjoyed among the *ancients*. Thus the nineteenth century acknowledged reborn 'classical' antiquity as the protagonist of the fifteenth and sixteenth centuries, and argued in turn that those centuries were crucial in the formation of 'modern man' or, to use an expression coined much later, 'Western civilization'.

During the twentieth century, historians worked hard to produce many more renaissances, such as the 'Renaissance of Frederick II' in the thirteenth century, 'The Renaissance of the Twelfth Century' which was the title of Charles Haskins's famous book (1927), the 'Ottonian Renaissance' around 1000 AD, the Carolingian Renaissance in Western Europe during the early Middle Ages, the Macedonian Renaissance in the East, the Northumbrian or Anglo-Saxon Renaissance in the North, and the Lombard Renaissance under King Liutprand. Modern scholarship has been studying these various rebirths and how they related to Antiquity and each other, especially since Erwin Panofsky first put his theories forward in *Renaissance and Renascences in Western Art* (1944, 2/1960). This argument was often revisited in order to identify the criteria for distinguishing between *the* Renaissance and the 'minor' renaissances. This sequence of rebirths can be interpreted in two ways: according to the continuative model there are not so much 'rebirths' as a continuing 'survival' of antiquity, which may be more or less pronounced in different epochs; according to the opposing model which emphasizes the discontinuity, 'classical' antiquity dies, is reborn and then dies again in cycles that continue up until the triumph of the 'real' Renaissance in fifteenth- and sixteenth-century Italy. In both cases, the absence of the 'classical' is associated with death, and its presence with life, in the particularly intense form of *new* life. 'Renaissance' and 'classical' are guiding ideas in European cultural history and their destinies are inextricably intertwined. Their development becomes a parallel development, as the Renaissance derives from the 'classical' and is indeed its rebirth, and therefore the Renaissance cannot fail to be 'classical' as well. Hence Raphael was to join the ancients as one of the 'perpetual' models to be imitated. The 'classical' is the protagonist of this *Vie des Formes* that has survived the passing centuries. It would reach perfection and then die, only to be reborn again and again. But the crucial historical problem, as we shall see (chapter 13), is precisely the plurality and *repeatability* of these resurrections.

11   The 'Classical' before 'Classical Antiquity'

Winckelmann did not use the term 'classical' to describe the antiquity we call 'classical', nor did Ghiberti, Vasari or any other writers from the fifteenth century to the eighteenth. Although the word 'classical' began to circulate in the sixteenth and seventeenth centuries, its use as a synonym for Graeco-Roman antiquity was not firmly established until the early nineteenth century. Before then, the terms 'ancient' and 'modern' were mainly used for contrasting or comparing the Greeks and Romans with contemporary experiences and projects. The debate on what would much later be called 'classical' naturally centred on these two terms. For this reason, any analysis of the meanings of the term 'classical' (even within a brief outline such as this) has to take into consideration the manner in which it crossed over the ancient-modern dichotomy, and the uses to which it was put. It is against this background that, in terms of both similarity and coexistence, the very concept of the 'renaissance [rebirth] of antiquity' must be placed: for what was this project if not an attempt to create a new modern manner of interpreting the 'classical' by imitating 'classical' antiquity?

The word *modernus* already existed in the Latin of Cassiodorus (?490–?585 AD), but it wasn't until the thirteenth and fourteenth centuries that people started to create a polemical opposition between *antiqui* and *moderni*, initially in the area of scholasticism (for example, the *modernus* Occam against the *antiquus* Aristotle) and later in a wider religious context, as in the *devotio moderna* of Geert de Groote (fourteenth century), a new religiosity that insisted on the inner dimension of faith and prayer rather than the traditional outer forms of piety. For Petrarch and Boccaccio, scholastic philosophers were *moderni*, but the *antiqui* included not only Virgil and Caesar but also Cola di Rienzo with his dreams of the rebirth of ancient Rome in the medieval city of Rome. *Antiquus*, in this sense, was no longer a chronological label but rather denoted the presence of an ethical and political project that in the fourteenth century meant reviving the passions and virtues of the ancients. In the following century, Lorenzo Valla shifted the comparison between the *antiqui* and *moderni*, now an almost obligatory exercise for men of learning, onto the terrain of the purity of the Latin language, and contrasted the barbarity of the *moderni* with the purity of the *antiqui*, the clumsy medieval Latin with the elegance of 'classical' Latin. Naturally this polemical analysis of language implied that whoever knew how to write good Latin (as he could) by following in the steps of the 'classics' fully merited the name of *antiquus*. In other words, the 'classical' identified not only the root, but also and above all, the project and the goal.

In all these cases, as in many other similar ones, the contrast referred to different models, positions and projects that were all entirely *contemporary*. Therefore the values of the two terms could be inverted according to the context: Occam and Groote could proudly claim to be *moderni* because they were convinced that they had improved upon the *antiqui*, while Valla believed that the *antiqui* in the sense of authors of 'classical' Latin were superior to *moderni*, as were contemporaries who knew how to write like those authors and could therefore also be referred to as *antiqui*. In the first case, the innovators were called *moderni*, and in the second, they were called *antiqui*, inverting the positive and negative associations, because in those particular generations, updating Latin writing meant imitation of the ancients. The

first application of these two opposing terms to the figurative
arts perhaps occurred when Giovanni Dondi dell'Orologio
(1375) contrasted the *moderni* (contemporary sculptors)
with the *antiqui* whose works were being dug up amongst
Roman ruins. Shortly afterwards Cennino Cennini wrote that
Giotto 'transformed the art of painting from the Greek [i.e.
Byzantine] to the Latin and made it modern' (*Libro dell'arte*,
c.1390). 'Greek' here is the Byzantine style, hallowed but
immobile, while 'Latin' means the new style introduced by
Giotto in line with the innovations arising from the study of
the ancient perceived as something essentially Romano-Latin
(for Cennino did not have the vaguest idea of what Greek
'classical' might have looked like). On this basis, artists who
practised the 'modern manner' were later referred to as *moderni*, although Vasari would insist that they were only such in
as much as they were steeped in the ancient and sustained by
an antiquarian sensitivity. Thus it could be said that an artist
was 'modernly ancient and anciently modern' (Anton
Francesco Doni said this of Vasari, and Vasari and Pietro
Aretino repeated it in connection with Giulio Romano).

   This concept implied a very clear distinction between the
ancient Greeks and Romans (the antiquity that would later
be referred to as 'classical') and modernity (the era that
would later be referred to as the 'Renaissance'). These were
almost opposites, in order that constant comparison could
become possible. As a result of this distinction, *antiquitas*,
which over many long centuries had been considered a lively
and contemporary source of norms and current thinking, was
transformed into a remote and finite *vetustas*, whose once
unchallengeable *auctoritas* did become more established, it is
true, but it also became open to once unthinkable compar-
isons, because it was more closely examined and was
therefore less elusive. Given that there was a long interval
between them, the resulting historical periodization con-
sisted of three ages, with an intervening age of an uncertain
nature. Seventeenth-century scholars coined a new word to
indicate it, *anticomoderno*, and it expressed the manner in
which it was balanced between two more clearly defined

ages (Federici, 2005). But another term was to prevail, that of *media tempestas*, which exists to this day in the form 'Middle Ages', an age that existed between two others, which had a preferential and almost exclusively polar relationship with each other. Thus the Middle Ages could not have been conceived as an historical period without the 'classical' and its proud and much acclaimed 'rebirth': the Renaissance.

During the seventeenth century, the *moderni* came to the conclusion that they had now entirely 'digested' the *antiqui*, and could challenge them for the position of superiority. Thus they abandoned the *antiqui* with their remote and finite antiquity, and created a new modernity, in which 'classical' culture was merely one of many ingredients. This gave rise to the 'Quarrel of the Ancients and the Moderns' which, in spite of many precedents such as the disputation between Coluccio Salutati and Nicolò Niccoli in Leonardo Bruni's *Dialogi* (*c.*1402), took its most accomplished form in France in the sixteenth and seventeenth centuries. Charles Perrault (1688) argued that the progressive accumulation of knowledge guaranteed the superiority of the moderns over the ancients. In his *Observations sur la statue de Marc Aurèle* (1771), the sculptor Étienne Falconet criticized the statue in the Capitol, which until then had been the undisputed model for every equestrian monument, and convinced himself that he had surpassed it in his statue of Peter the Great in St Petersburg (1766–82). However this work was indebted to the work of G. L. Bernini on an equestrian statue of Louis XIV which was not favourably received by its subject. Of course, there was no shortage of fierce and elaborate counter-arguments, but the very fact that the superiority of the ancients or the moderns was up for discussion demonstrated that the authority of the ancients was no longer so settled and unassailable. And it was during this famous *querelle* that the rare word *classicus* was unearthed from Latin literature and started to circulate in European languages.

In Latin, the term *classicus* was not coined to define phenomena and eras from cultural history; it belonged to political and economic discourse (it was related to the six *classes* of Roman citizens laid down in the Servian Constitution). *Classicus* came to mean in its most restricted sense a citizen belonging to the highest *classis* of taxpayers. It was not until the second century AD that Aulus Gellius used it figuratively to describe a writer as 'classicus scriptor, non proletarius' – 'of the first order' and not 'one of the mass' (*Noctes atticae* 19.8.15; see also 6.13.1 and 16.10.2–15) and, perhaps even more aptly, 'good for being read by the *classici* (the richest taxpayers), but not by the people'. *Classicus* was also defined as *adsiduus* (another term concerning wealth, 'a solid and frequent taxpayer') and *antiquior*, which suggests that a pedigree was a requirement for being 'classical'. Such a definition reflected the grammarians' passion for classification. They identified a restricted list of 'obligatory' or 'chosen' (*enkrithentes* in Greek) authors for each genre in the immense corpus of Greek literature: for example, Aeschylus, Sophocles and Euripides amongst the tragedians. These lists were referred to in Greek as *pinakes* (tables) and in Latin, particularly from Quintilian onwards, as those of *ordo* (rank or methodical arrangement) or *numerus* (number). It was David Ruhnken who first applied the Greek term *kanon* (rule or model) to them in 1768. Previously – since Eusebius in the fourth century – *kanon* had designated the list of books in the Bible that the Church considered to have been inspired. It should not surprise us therefore that Gellius introduced the term *classicus scriptor* in the context of his analysis of controversial grammatical forms, for which, he argued, the usage of an established author had to act as the norm (E. R. Curtius).

However, the Middle Ages did not use *classicus* as one of the terms for the unchallenged *auctoritas* of the ancients. The word, as adopted by Gellius, came back into use in the sixteenth century, initially, it would appear, in French and then in other European languages, and it only applied to literary texts. Thus there were 'classical' writers in the sixteenth and seventeenth centuries, but there were no 'classical' statues; nor was there a 'classical antiquity'. Even more significant is the fact that the term 'classical' in modern European languages was in no way restricted to Greek and Latin authors (nor had it ever been). It could be applied to any text that was considered to be exemplary, even in a modern language. This meaning soon became overlaid with another, associated with a modern educational use of the Latin word *classis* and its derivations in European languages: 'classical' also came to mean 'that which is studied in class'. In France particularly, the word *classique* identified the works and authors of French literature considered to set the norm (the first recorded example of this usage appears to be in Thomas Sebillet's *Art poétique* of 1548, which states that 'les bons et classiques poètes françois' are Jean de Meun of the thirteenth century and Alain Chartier of the fifteenth). The term became common usage after the foundation of the Académie Française in 1635. A similar but less frequent and codified usage also started to appear in Italian and English in the seventeenth century.

The models *par excellence* came from Greek and Latin literature, and therefore some of their works were occasionally defined as 'classical' but without creating a separate category, as that remained the exclusive domain of the term 'ancients' (or *anciens*). Latin authors were referred to as 'classical' when they could instruct how to reproduce a Latin free from medieval 'barbarism'. Greek writers could earn the definition if they were considered indispensable to the recovery of an antiquity no longer understood as exclusively Roman, an attitude that had been around since 1533, when the *praeceptor Germaniae* Melanchthon had started to claim the superiority of Greek writers over Latin ones. He was soon to be joined by many others of the same opinion. Thus the idea of the 'classical' took form in Europe by taking from Greek and Roman Antiquity both the term and the desire to seek out prescriptive models for the present, and contained an inner contradiction that would influence all its further developments. And this occurred at the same time that the *Querelle des Anciens et des Modernes* questioned whether such models were only to be sought out in antiquity. 'Classical' could therefore be an ancient model or a more recent one belonging to a national culture. In the latter case, literature could be worthy of the designation 'classical' either because it adhered perfectly to Graeco-Roman models or, for the opposite reason, because it had managed to better or push aside those models and create a new set of norms *ex nihilo*.

Although only literary texts were referred to as 'classical' at the time, artists and architects were diligently studying the damaged artworks of antiquity. They did not call their models 'classical', but they spoke with reverence of the ancients. They knew Roman works and cherished the hope of discovering Greek works which Latin sources themselves acknowledged as superior. Occasionally these early modern artists and architects would consider sculptures of the highest quality to be 'of Greek chisel', and were universally and deeply moved by the discovery of the Greek *Laocoön* amongst the ruins of Rome (1506). However, their praise partly resulted from their having read in Pliny that it had once been kept in the home of the Roman emperor Titus. At the same time, antiquarianism was becoming a more clearly defined discipline and was gaining in status. It set itself the task of tenderly gathering together the fragments of that *sacrosancta antiquitas* the centuries had broken up and dispersed, and gave equal weight to oil-lamps, Livy's text, an incomplete epigraph and the *Apollo di Belvedere*. For every tiny element contributed to the study and reconstruction of antiquity which had been defiled and dispersed by centuries of neglect.

Thus they created a fertile mix of two factors that today appear mutually exclusive and alien to each other: artistic practice which for centuries governed the perception of the ancient and the antiquarians' encyclopaedic and analytical calling. The process was already clearly established at the time of Raphael, a brilliant artist but also a careful surveyor of Roman ruins working for Leo X, and reached its supreme moment of synthesis with Rubens, who was not only the 'new Apelles' but also a collector of antiquities and a consummate antiquarian. Antiquarian scholarship drew sustenance and encouragement from the attention artists paid to the ancient, and artists perceived the study of 'classical' objects and customs not as a dispassionate and bookish pastime but as a refreshing attention to the truth entirely in the quest for an aesthetics of *convenevolezza* or seemliness requiring 'archaeological' faithfulness to the details of history painting. In Rome, Cassiano Dal Pozzo was using a small army of artists to build up his extremely ambitious *Museo cartaceo* (Paper Museum), an early attempt to create a general corpus of antiquities recorded by drawings. On the basis of a very similar antiquarian culture, the greatest of his painter friends, Nicolas Poussin, was intent upon his own study of the ancient marbles of Rome in order to learn how to depict humanity in 'classical' dress through gestures full of ritual eloquence and intense and controlled warmth.

In the late eighteenth and nineteenth centuries, this trend was reversed and, in spite of the best efforts of Winckelmann and Mengs, there was a divorce between antiquarianism and artistic practice. The planned reassembly of the ancient was channelled into the university system and its disciplines. This was the point in which 'classical antiquity' could be invented and enshrined in academic discourse. This brought in such terms as 'classical philology', 'classical archaeology', museums of 'classical' art, *klassische Altertumswissenschaft* (science of classical antiquity), and departments of 'classical' studies. Because the new universities needed to classify disciplines and set them in order of importance, they also needed to distinguish Graeco-Roman antiquity from other antiquities such as the Jewish and Egyptian ones. However, the decision to define it as 'classical' implied that it was the model and therefore dominant antiquity. The manifesto for founding this discipline of ancient studies was F. A. Wolf 's *Darstellung der Alterthums-Wissenschaft* (1807), which created a complex structure for the science of antiquity and divided it into twenty-four disciplines. That programme, which agreed with many of Wilhelm von Humboldt's ideas, inspired the increasing role of 'classical' culture not only in antiquarian and literary studies but also more generally in the education of ruling elites. Analogous developments and the spread of ideas led to similar conclusions in the whole of Europe. In full and perhaps unconscious accordance with Gellius' metaphor (based on distinctions between taxpayers), the new 'classical' culture was aimed at the modern-day *classici*, the ruling and upper middle classes (in opposition to the *proletarii* as it had been with Gellius). Just as educational systems had long placed the study of Latin and Greek on a pedestal, so museums from London to Berlin wanted to boast the presence of marbles taken from Athens or Pergamum and made casts for artists to use as models. There was an incessant emphasis on the identity between the European tradition and the ancients, who were the fathers and educators of that civilization.

There were, however, many contradictions in the use of the word 'classical', and they continue to exist. Firstly, as we have seen, a single word, 'classical', can mean either the whole of Graeco-Roman antiquity or only a part of it (typically the fifth and fourth centuries BC or the Athens of Pericles). Nor do the possible variants end here: there are geographical variants such as Greek art in Sicily of the fifth century BC, which is sometimes defined as 'anti-classical' (see chapter 6), and there are profound distinctions that concern different fields, such as the 'classical' era for law, which is that of Ulpian, Papinian and Paulus, namely the Severian age art historians consider to be decidedly post-'classical' or 'late classical'. In spite of its enormous success, the more general definition of a Graeco-Roman 'classical' antiquity has not precluded attempts to restrict the meaning of the 'classical' (e.g. the Greek as against the Roman, or early Greek art as against the 'classical' in its more restricted sense; see chapter 6). Other problems of terminology were highlighted by Władisław Tatarkiewicz (1958), who distinguished four different meanings of the word 'classical':

a)   When it denotes value, 'classical' can stand for 'first class', perfect and acknowledged model (in contrast with the imperfect and mediocre);

b)   When it denotes a chronological period, 'classical' is a synonym for 'Graeco-Roman antiquity' (or simply

Greek civilization at its height: in this sense, Tatarkiewicz points out, it would be quite possible to argue that of the three tragic poets of the canon, Aeschylus *is not yet* 'classical', and Euripides *is no longer* 'classical';

c) When it denotes an historical style, 'classical' refers to modern writers, artists and others who wish to conform with ancient models;

d) When it denotes an aesthetic category, 'classical' refers to authors and works associated with harmony, moderation and balance.

Moreover, 'classical' could also be defined as one element in a series of opposites: in the sixteenth and seventeenth centuries it was contrasted with the 'Gothic' (i.e. medieval art), in the nineteenth century it was contrasted with the 'Romantic' (and also the Baroque by art historians), and in the twentieth century it was contrasted with the 'primitive' (although it would perhaps be more appropriate to call this the 'authentic').

Of Tatarkiewicz's four meanings, only one (b) has been examined in this book. However, it is only where it intersects with the other meanings that the profound influence of the 'classical', its invincible vitality and the multiplicity of its properties becomes fully apparent. I have used the word 'classical' (always in inverted commas) even when referring to eras in which the word was not used with this meaning, because even then the same concept was being formed under another name ('ancient'). This concept then took on the name of 'classical' and permeated Europe's educational systems and shared culture. When 'classical' was definitively defined in order to create a clearly demarcated academic discipline to cover all 'classical' (i.e. Graeco-Roman) antiquity, the noble and prestigious word for use in universities, grammar schools and their curricula was chosen because it raised 'classical' education to the pinnacle of all educational systems and made it the cultural idiom in which elites of many countries, nations and languages could identify with each other.

The concurrent developments of the modern terms 'classical' and 'Renaissance' were part of this context. Both took on their present meanings between the 1770s and the Restoration, and both became fully part of the institutional and academic framework during the first half of the nineteenth century. This was entirely logical, because the Renaissance, which was perceived in the nineteenth and twentieth centuries as the dawn of 'modern European man', was defined by its protagonists as a *renovatio* of ('classical') antiquity. 'Classical' and 'Renaissance' therefore have a symmetrical relationship: one could never have existed without the other, and one could not be explained without the other.

Another question now arises: did the ancient Greeks and Romans have their own 'classical' era? Or perhaps we should ask whether the ancients had their own Antiquity. This question is not anachronistic, although it may initially appear so. While it is true that we cannot expect Greek and Latin texts to contain a fully worked-out definition of the 'classical' in the sense it has acquired over the last two centuries, it is also true that Graeco-Roman Antiquity, which we call 'classical', did develop at its very core a retrospective self-perception that it passed onto successive generations all the way down to our own, as an integral part of its legacy.

As we have seen (chapters 7 and 8), Winckelmann's historical narrative portrayed the development of Greek art (and civilization in general) as the parabola of human life. Thus he attributed art with a tentative infancy, a pure youth, a fruitful middle age and then a slow decline into old age until overtaken by death. However Winckelmann only put flesh on an historical model that already existed: simplified versions can be found in writings on art as far back as the Renaissance, particularly in Italy. The first, in fact, was Lorenzo Ghiberti's *Commentarii* (*c*.1450). Winckelmann took this evolutionary model from Vasari's *Lives* and above all Joseph Scaliger's *Thesaurus temporum* (1606), with its rich seam of ancient sources, and adapted it to the artistic tastes of his own time.

It is easy to explain the like-mindedness of Ghiberti, Vasari, Scaliger, Winckelmann and many others: they had all read Pliny the Elder, in particular the last books of the *Natural History*, which provide the only extant summary of the history of ancient art based on extensive reading of Greek treatises on art that have since been lost. Pliny was not alone, as Vitruvius also structured his accounts of artists and architects in accordance with this biological parabola of flowering and decadence, which besides was frequently used in ancient sources for the history of rhetoric and poetry (e.g. Cicero and Quintilian).

Pliny did not, however, invent his parabolic model; he took it from Greek sources, particularly two authors from the third century BC, Xenocrates of Athens and Antigonus of Carystus, sculptors who also wrote on the history of art. They placed themselves and their era on the downward trajectory of the parabola, and therefore had already developed a retrospective perception based on admiration of an antiquity that was superior to the present and in a sense already 'classical' (if we are to impose our own classification). Traces of this interpretation can be found in other writers on art, such as Duris of Samos (who was not however a professional artist). The biological-evolutionary paradigm was not invented for the development of art, as it took form in the Aristotelian school, which inspired the composition of specialist narratives for such disciplines as medicine, rhetoric, music, geometry, and so on (not just sculpture and painting), with particular attention being paid to chronology and the principle of historical evolution. This was the principle that occasioned Aristotle's extraordinarily forceful and effective account of the development of tragedy in the *Poetics*: tragedy was created through improvisation, gradually developed as poets explored its potential, underwent numerous changes, and eventually reached its most complete form at the point where its development halted. Thus historical narrative, which had already been applied to politics, was also applied to particular fields, especially those of the *technai* (medicine, architecture, etc.). One of Aristotle's disciples, Dicaearchus of Messina, had the singular idea of writing a *Life of Greece* in which an essentially cultural history of the Greeks was represented as a biological parabola as though it were the *cursus vitae* of a single individual, but unlike the Aristotelian history of tragedy which stopped when it reached its highpoint and moment of greatest maturity, Dicaearchus introduced a final catastrophe as the end of the parabola. In the biological analogy this catastrophic end corresponds to an individual death. This idea of forcing an entire arc of historical development into the model of a human life – from infancy to death – did not remain an isolated attempt, but was taken up by the greatest of Roman scholars, Marcus Terentius Varro, in his *Vita Populi Romani*, which was undoubtedly known to Pliny the Elder.

Pliny therefore had two excellent reasons for adopting this biological-evolutionary paradigm for the figurative arts: the Dicaearchus model (filtered through Varro at the very least) and his sources specific to the history of art, such as Xenocrates of Athens. Thus the biographical model of history (and of the history of art) contributed decisively to the way ancient art was perceived, and through Pliny it would influence all modern writers on art from Ghiberti onwards, while Winckelmann became its most coherent and eloquent exponent. However, the idea that the highpoint of Greek civilization was already in the past had had enormous currency throughout the period between the fourth or third century BC and the early centuries of the Empire. Historians and rhetoricians were recommending the use of Thucydides' language and method rather than those of the present, and artists increasingly revived or reworked models based on the works of Phidias and Polyclitus in such a conspicuous manner that archaeologists have defined much of the sculpture of the Hellenistic age as 'neoclassical'. Neo-Attic and neo-archaic (or archaistic) styles were invented and spread during this era; they put forward the figurative and stylistic methods that belonged to a few centuries previous and appeared to want to ignore or repress the experiences of later generations in the name of an uncontainable and anguished nostalgia for the times of the great masters.

This cult of the past soon created new Roman collectors, who avidly sought great works of the past for exhibition either in public spaces or at home. When it came to contemporary art, they preferred it to be close to the styles of the prestigious age (primarily from Polyclitus to Lysippus). There were two particularly important developments during this late Hellenistic and Roman period: first came the birth of 'history of art' as a literary genre, which had a markedly nostalgic outlook (we know the general tenor mainly through Pliny the Elder's meagre summary), and then came the boom in a vast industry of copies of 'classical' sculptures (just at the time that artistic historiography was coming to an end, after having created its own canons). Casts were made and then copied in marble and bronze with sufficient faithfulness for buyers to recognize a work by Polyclitus in copies of the *Doryphorus* and a work by Myron in copies of the *Discobolos*. This was a new phenomenon: copying is not an obvious practice (indeed it is restricted to very few civilizations), and presupposes a public that is anxious to own prestigious (highly 'classical') art, where the originals are unattainable. It should be noted in passing that this taste and this mass production had an unforeseen result: once all the Greek originals had disappeared, it was only possible to know artists such as Polyclitus and Myron through copies (recovered through the analysis of 'philological' archaeology; see chapter 6).

It is impossible to understand the enormous success of an interpretative model of history (or history of art) based on such a radical belittlement of the present in relation to the past, without reference to the decisive context of political history. For some, as far back as the fifth century BC in Athens, the catastrophic outcome of the Peloponnesian Wars triggered a sense of decadence in the city's fortunes, and also forms of nostalgia for a very recent past (for example the return of Aeschylus' plays to the stage). In any event, yearning for the 'classical' form of the *polis* and the ideas of citizenship, community and autonomy made itself felt in Greece very soon after the loss of political initiative (from the fourth century BC onwards) had undermined not only the bases of the *polis* of the old regime (i.e. the idea of the armed citizenry), but also the new ideal of the *koiné eirene* ('shared peace') of all Greeks, which had been expressed in Andocides' speech of 391–390 BC, *De Pace*. The new elites of the Greek cities were based on wealth, the mobility of capital and the manipulation of consensus in accordance with powerful Greek sovereigns and later the Romans. It can be argued that the universal nostalgia amongst intellectuals, artists and their patrons for the past greatness of Greeks in literature and the arts reflected the widespread sense of the *poleis* (Athens in particular) having been marginalized from the great political events of the day and of their dramatic 'loss of liberty' (i.e. the right to self-government). This was matched by a sense that they had also lost the intimate link between the art of such men as Sophocles and Phidias to the 'classical' form of the *polis*. It is in this light that we must interpret the gesture of Roman consul Titus Quinctius Flamininus following his defeat of the Macedonian king, Philip V, at the Battle of Cynoscephalae and his subjugation of Greece to Rome: he solemnly announced at the Isthmian Games of 196 BC that Rome would restore to Greece its liberty and the *koiné eirene*. It was, in its own way, a nostalgic and 'classicist' gesture, or rather he was able to play on the widespread nostalgic or 'classicist' sentiments of the Greeks. His considerable political intuition managed to exploit those sentiments in the interests of Rome by presenting the arrival of a new conqueror as liberation from the old. Thus the 'classicism' of the ancients owes as much to politics as it does to culture and art.

Two other considerations need to be made. The first is that the existence at a particular stage in history of 'classics' for the ancients justifies all modern attempts to identify a more restricted period within the long development of 'classical' antiquity that merits being considered more genuinely and intensely 'classical' than the other periods, and this has tended to put the spotlight on fifth-century Athens. The second is that the idea of a Renaissance or rebirth of art (following its death), which was and is so pervasive, would have been unthinkable without the paradigmatic biological parabola the ancients developed and handed down to modernity. Aristotle suggested that 'it is likely that every art and every philosophy has been discovered and developed to its full on many occasions, only to be lost once again' (*Metaphysics* XII, 1074b). However, the ancients never fully formulated a model of historical development based on rebirth following a 'death' of culture and art. It was only in the modern age that the model of the biological parabola was taken to its ultimate conclusion: the final stage of the evolutionary paradigm of ancient art was used, on Pliny's authority, to exalt fifteenth- and sixteenth-century Italian art. As the arts were dead at the end of antiquity, they could be reborn, and were in fact reborn. The concept of the history of art used by ancient writers, which was transmitted down the generations by Pliny in a summarized but recognizable form, thus became profoundly absorbed into our thinking and put to new purposes. The model of the biological parabola which ends in decadence and the death of the arts became, with the addition of the rebirth, a cyclical model that tends towards infinite repetition through a succession of cultural catastrophes and rebirths.

The root of the symmetry between 'classical' and 'Renaissance' (as mentioned in chapters 10 and 11) is to be found precisely here in the dark abyss that separates death and resurrection. Although it was not until the nineteenth century that these concepts took on their current meanings in a clearly defined academic and institutional context, they were however based on a premise that would have been clearly understood by Petrarch's generation: the need to return to the ancients, revive them and make them relevant to modern times by contrasting them with the moderns. Indeed the task was to become like the ancients in order to understand them in depth, relive their experiences and reintroduce their teachings. They then sought out the 'classical' in the Rome of Augustus rather than the Athens of Pericles, but they had introduced a mechanism that was to recur throughout Western cultural history: the desire to legitimize the present in terms of the 'correct' models of the past, no matter whether those models were Augustus or Pericles, Virgil or Sophocles, the grace of the *Apollo di Belvedere*, the pain expressed in the *Laocoön* or the austere purity of an ancient torso. But this mechanism was triggered overridingly by the idea of a return to the past that came from the very heart of antiquity itself: the Greek sources of art history (read in Pliny's compendium) and Roman copies of Greek master-pieces. These ideas filter into any modern ideal of the 'classical' precisely because they were themselves born as a form of ancient 'classicism'.

Unlike us, the ancients did not have a word to codify the 'classical'. Gellius' isolated *classicus* does not change this. It is entirely typical that Plutarch (second century AD), in order to define the works on the Acropolis created under Pericles' patronage as the supreme artistic achievement, claimed that each one 'was immediately *ancient* even then *because of its beauty*, but today they appear so fresh, as though they had just been finished. They seem to possess an eternal youth that protects them from the assaults of time, almost as though they were filled with a spirit that blossoms unendingly and a soul incapable of ageing' (*Life of Pericles*, 13.3).

A scholar of our own time has translated *kallei archaion*, which appears in this passage (literally 'ancient because of beauty') as 'classic in its perfection' (Griffin 1989). It is a modernizing translation – it is true – but quite appropriate in its attempt to condense the meaning into one word, and what Plutarch and his heirs (right down to the present day) read from the Parthenon can only be defined as 'classical'. Thus modernity can with a certain justification read between the lines of antiquity and come up with a word the ancients did not possess. The antiquity of the ancients, with its drive to endorse and judge the present through a powerful nostalgia for the past, summoned up and indeed moulded all *our* images of Antiquity – all our 'classicisms'.

13   Eternity amongst the Ruins

As art's death-rebirth sequence was handed down over generations from Ghiberti to Winckelmann and then to twentieth-century historians, it revealed its unrivalled interpretative fruitfulness, and its repeatability *ad infinitum* became one of its essential characteristics. The biological model of history, which was born to interpret cultural history through a man's individual life, ended up dramatically differentiating itself from such a life. A man dies and is not reborn, whereas the 'classical' dies in order to be reborn, and on each occasion it is the same as it was before and yet also different. This cyclical model, this recurring obsession with a 'classical' which is always given up for dead and is always reborn, is present throughout European cultural history. Consequently the rebirths become increasingly numerous. We encountered some examples in chapter 10, but we can add others by looking to the eastern half of the ancient empire and even further back. In the Byzantine context, specialists have identified not only a 'Macedonian renaissance', but also a 'Comnenian renaissance', a 'Palaeologian renaissance' (names based on the imperial dynasties) and even a 'pre-Macedonian renaissance', which coincided with the iconoclastic age. However, we can keep going even further back, and there is talk of rebirths in the ages of Justinian and of Theodosius. As Alexander Kazhdan (1988) has observed, the cultural history of

Byzantium can be 'seen as an endless Rebirth divided into stages ... In practice, these Rebirths cover the entirety of the Byzantine millennium. But don't the ideas of continuity and Rebirth contradict each other?' Even historians of Graeco-Roman 'classical' art have identified rebirths (or 'classicistic' phases) within its development – for example the ages of Augustus, Hadrian and Gallienus. According to Rodenwaldt (1931), there was an even earlier renaissance of the 'classical' in the Hellenistic Age.

As can be seen from this bald and incomplete list, the concept of rebirth, having been created to define *the* Renaissance, became a pervasive classification of value applied retrospectively by analogy to other ages and cultural processes. As Kazhdan's extremely pertinent pronouncement implies, the persistent use and re-use of this category creates an unending and unresolved alternation between models based on continuity and models based on various degrees of discontinuity. It also implies a very idiosyncratic status for the 'classical' as a category, because it arises from different classifications and historical analyses. It should indeed be said that the 'classical' takes on a different and particular form not only in relation to its every real and supposed rebirth, but also every time it is mentioned by specialists as a category for historical interpretation: on the one hand, the 'classical' of the Carolingian Renaissance is different from the Palaeologian or the Sicilian and southern Italian renaissance under the Holy Roman Emperor Frederick II, and on the other, Khazdan's 'classical' is different from Haskins's or Panofsky's. Equally Le Corbusier's 'classical' is different from Bofill's (see chapter 4), and even now it would be easy to find and describe many different definitions, concepts and uses of the 'classical' within a single year. It could be argued that these say more about the people who put them forward than about the innumerable aspects of the basic concept and its semantic uses. The analysis of the variants of the 'classical' relates not only to cultural history of the past but also to our intellectual outlook in the present.

The regular and intermittent recourse to forms of the

'classical' in order either to understand the past or to engage with the present have taken on hundreds of variants since Greek culture first glorified itself by promoting a cult of its own past, and this now constitutes an historical phenomenon so unusual that Ernst Howald (1948) was able to argue that the rebirth of the 'classical' is a 'rhythmical form' within European cultural history. Howald's analysis perceives the unrelenting cyclical return of the 'classical', rather than the 'classical' itself, as the principal feature of our cultural memory. This immediately raises the question of whether this 'rhythmical form' is peculiar to the Western tradition, and if so, why. This question is intimately wound up with our perception of the damaged artworks of Antiquity, whose relentless decay bears witness to both their demise and their past existence. In other words, they demonstrate the death of Antiquity and herald its rebirth. The ruins are themselves a powerful metaphoric embodiment and a tangible demonstration of both the demise of an ancient world and its intermittent and cyclical reawakenings. Thus the sentiments aroused by ruins, so central to the European cultural memory since the Middle Ages, can be used in this context as a kind of litmus test.

For the Western tradition, ruins denote both a presence and an absence: they demonstrate, indeed *they are*, the point where the visible and the invisible meet. That which is invisible (or absent) is summoned up and accentuated by the fragmentation of ruins, their 'useless' and occasionally incomprehensible nature and their loss of purpose (or at least their original purpose). However their obstinate visible presence demonstrates, far more than their loss of utility, the longevity and indeed eternity of ruins and their victory over the ineluctable course of time. The saying attributed to Bede ('As long as the Coliseum survives, so will Rome, and as long as Rome survives, so will the world') was not a reference to the Coliseum in its heyday, a place whose performances attracted hundreds of thousands of spectators, but rather to its existence as a gigantic ruin that then as now continued to die in every instant and yet continued to live.

Not only do ruins challenge time, they also inspire reflections and reactions. Thus they can be looked upon and acquire status in their new codified role as precisely what they have become – ruins.

As Chateaubriand argued in a famous passage from *Génie du Christianisme* (1802), 'all men feel a secret attraction towards ruins', because of a sense of the sublime evoked by the contrast between our human condition and the fall of great empires, to which the ruins bear witness. But perhaps Chateaubriand was wrong, and that attraction or feeling is peculiar to culture in the European tradition. Perhaps ruins, the symbol of a faded past that is still present, are closely linked to that sequence of small and large rebirths, the regular death and reawakening of antiquity. It could be argued that this peculiarity (if such it is) was ultimately moulded by an event that left its indelible mark on the history and cultural memory of what we call the West: the sudden, traumatic rift caused by the fall of Rome. If we are thinking of Romulus Augustulus and the date 476 AD, which only history textbooks consider to be fateful, then it really was 'the inaudible fall of an empire', as Momigliano (1980) defined it. Yet the slow process of that fall, the lingering death throes that commenced centuries beforehand, did involve a dramatic break with the past: the more or less contemporaneous (and definitive) collapse of a religion, a state and territorial organization, and a society with its own institutions, values, and cultural and behavioural paradigms. What remained became inextricably fused with the thoughts, values and memories of the Judaeo-Christian tradition. Although there have been rifts and discontinuities in the histories of all peoples, nothing in the other great cultural traditions of India, China and Japan quite compares with this 'end of the ancient world' (partly because of the magnitude of the stage on which it occurred).

A study by Wu Hung (1995) allows us to make a brief comparison with China. It appears that the sense of attachment to ruins has no place in Chinese culture. Paintings of ruins only appear very rarely and very late, and are by painters that were to some extent influenced by Europe, such as

Fan Qi (1616–94). No narrative scene was ever set against a backdrop of ruins, nor was there any representation of a man visiting, observing and reflecting upon ruins. A traditional genre of Chinese poetry called *huaigu* (meditation on or lament for the past) would appear to lend itself to descriptions of ruins and reflections on them, but in reality it never produced anything comparable with the European tradition. Two words, which signify two fundamental concepts, are suitable for discussing ruins: *xu* and *ji*. *Xu* means 'vacuum', 'desolation', 'destruction', and can be found in some *huaigu*, as well as paintings also belonging to the *huaigu* genre, and these contain the poetic experiences and meditations of travellers. But the 'ruins' mentioned in the texts or depicted in the paintings are never abandoned buildings but rather uncultivated fields and dying trees: in other words, ruins of nature and not of human constructions. The other concept, *ji*, refers to ruins as 'traces' of something else, particularly historical figures. As Wu Hung writes, 'whereas *xu* emphasizes the cancellation or concealment of all traces of mankind, *ji* demonstrates their survival and display'. For these purposes, anything (a hill, tree, river or temple) could become *ji* once an association has been established with an event or person from the past. Once again, however, the artworks deal in the great majority of cases with elements of a natural landscape rather than ruins. Only in a few cases immediately following the fall of the Ming dynasty did painters depict scenes such as a *Visit to a Stele*. These steles had commemorative inscriptions to Ming officials; they were evocations of the past, but the steles were set in the landscape and depicted as perfectly intact and not damaged (although the inscription is not always legible). In these images, the passing of time is not represented by the steles, but by the twisted and withered trees in a 'ruinous' state. Once again, the *pathos* of time and history is entrusted to nature and not to signs of culture. The steles denote the past but not the passing of time. Even Chinese antiquarians, who have a tradition much more ancient than Europeans have, did not collect steles but rather ink rubbings taken from them, as they were more interested in calligraphy.

This situation reflected other realities: many ancient trees were treated with reverence as they recorded events or historical figures (and when one of the trees died, another was immediately planted in the same place and would take on the same role even though it was not 'ancient'); ruined buildings, however, were never objects of veneration or reflection. If it was considered sufficiently important, a ruined building was rebuilt on the foundations in a manner that resembled the ancient one as closely as possible. If not, it was abandoned without regrets and removed from the historical and cultural memory. According to Wu Hung, this attitude is still very much alive (for example in the ruins created by Mao's Cultural Revolution), although there are a few, very few exceptions, all recent and resulting from the influence of Western culture. In short, ruined buildings of the past do not have a role in the cultural memory of China. The pathos of passing time is expressed by natural objects, whereas man-made objects, once abandoned, dissolve into nature and become indistinguishable from it. At this stage, the symbols that nature provides to describe decadence, ruin and the ineluctable passage of time are perceived as infinitely more powerful and occupy all available space.

Nature also has a significant role in the Western cultural perception of ruins. Indeed Georg Simmel argued that a ruin constitutes the synthesis between nature (principally understood as a destructive force) and culture, and 'a ruin's fascination is ultimately to be found in the realization that man's creations can be perceived as products of nature' (Simmel, ed. Wolff, 1959). But ruins can tell us things that natural objects cannot: they remind us of their ancient builders and users, but they also make us think about those who neglected, sacked and destroyed them. The fact that some of them have been conserved, visited and restored as ruins also reminds us of those who up until the present day have attempted to give a meaning in the here and now to those crumbling remnants of the past. In this, the tradition of Western Europe is distinct from the Byzantine one: there were of course ruins in the Eastern Empire, and sometimes (but very rarely) they were mentioned in texts but never depicted in art. As Byzantines called themselves *Rhomaioi* (Romans) and with justification considered themselves the legitimate successors of the Roman Empire, their sense of absolute and unquestionable continuity deprived the ruins of that pathos and the fullness of meaning we perceive in the West. Ruins were almost never understood as symbols of change from one age to another, not even after the two occasions on which Constantinople fell (the crusader invasion of 1204 and the Turkish one of 1453).

We can tentatively refer to a counter-argument concerning a much more remote context. The fall of the pre-Columbian empires in Mexico and Peru was comparable with the 'end of the ancient world' in Western Europe, in terms of its drastic and sudden transition from one world to another and from one religion to another. The civilizations overrun by the *conquistadores* left imposing ruins behind them, which only recently have regained their rightful fame. And yet we cannot speak of a preoccupation with ruins comparable with that of the European tradition. The reasons are exactly the opposite to those relating to the Byzantine civilization: there was what might be called an 'excess of continuity' in Byzantium (as in China), whereas there was an 'excess of discontinuity' in the forced transition from pre-Columbian America. In a few very particular situations this effect was lessened: for example, the last Mayan kingdoms resisted the Spanish until the beginning of the eighteenth century and the Hopi of Arizona rejected assimilation and have kept their religion alive until the present day. The nostalgia that the end of those civilizations undoubtedly generated did not have any means of expressing itself, nor was there any means of handing its own distinctive voice down the generations, precisely because of the sudden and radical elimination of anyone who could have developed that sentiment. When archaeologists rediscovered those ruins and started to study them very much later, the outlook was irredeemably that of archaeology in the European mould, itself a development from sixteenth- and seventeenth-century antiquarianism. In other words, there does not appear to be an 'indigenous' feeling for the ruins in this cultural environment, but simply an 'exogenous' one induced by the adoption of European cultural elements. For instance, Fernando de Alba Ixtlilxochitl (1568–1648), a mestizo with royal Aztec blood, did describe the ruins of the Texcoco Palace, which were also depicted in Quinatzin's map of about 1542 (Douglas 2003), but he did so from the viewpoint of his Europeanized and Christian educational background. He evoked the works and achievements of the Greeks and Romans, while claiming that those of the American peoples were no less significant, 'even though the passage of time and the destruction of my ancestors' states has plunged their history into obscurity'. This 'exogenous' and comparative approach to ruins is closer to the Chinese one than to the European, which is by its very nature 'endogenous'. The same can be said of Japan, where the depiction of ruins in relation to the history of the imperial family commenced around 1880, after the country opened up to Western influences.

Seemingly the sentiment attached to ruins (or, to put it another way, a complex discourse *on* ruins) is particular to Western culture, and it could be argued that it is not so much linked to the fall of empire in itself as to the unique balance between continuity and discontinuity following the collapse of the Roman Empire. This sentiment is principally embodied in ruins (because of their mix of presence and absence), but also extends to languages, behaviour, institutions, and the endless traces of the ancient, 'classical' culture we all often unwittingly carry around with us. This explanation is also valid for the periodic rebirth of the 'classical' as a 'rhythmical form', which is exclusive to European cultural history. However these cycles are the other side of the same coin, given that the rebirths always feed off fragments of the past (ruins) that are constantly poised between life and death. The pathos of one's own tradition is dominant in other civilizations, while in our civilization the pathos that dominates is for ruins, the incurable rift that has to be healed: rebirth as the indispensable condition for tradition and memory.

14   Identity and Otherness

In these cycles of reversions and rebirths, there are alterna-
tions between many contrasting manifestations of the
'classical' (which often do not use this name to define themselves). During the twentieth century, in which 'classical'
studies started on a high note and then gradually declined, we
can isolate two perceptions of the 'classical', which were not
actually born in opposition to each other, although they now
appear highly antithetical. The first, tendentially a-historical
option wished to perceive the 'classical' as an immutable and
perpetual system of universal values without place or time,
and these values were by a happy coincidence codified by the
Greeks, spread by the Romans and duly passed down to us.
The other perception attempted to historicize the 'classical'
by placing its various periods, as well as its contradictions and
internal differences, not only in the overall timeframe and
sequence of events, but also in a network of intercultural
relations. This means there was no immaculate origin but
rather a tree whose dense roots run deep and whose branches
are often broken or hidden from view. For this reason, there
were also attempts to compare its cyclical return with similar
phenomena in other cultures, as we shall see.

During the crucial interwar years, the differences of
emphasis, intensity and spirit between these two perceptions
continued but also became more polarized. At one extreme

on the a-historical side of the argument, there was massive exploitation of the 'classical' by totalitarian regimes, particularly in Italy and Germany. These regimes incorporated and promoted the tendency towards the 'authentic', albeit in a very simplified form – the primitive and regenerative form of the 'classical' that was inspiring the cultural scene at the time (see chapter 6). They then grafted this tendency onto a vitalistic and nationalistic context of their own. As a consequence, they promoted a vision of the 'classical' as the original depository of values, its presentation as perpetual and unchanging, and its *de facto* treatment as something that can be manipulated and simplified into schematic formulas at will. Given its prestigious place in the culture and educational systems of the elites, the 'classical' was adapted as an 'instrument for enchantment and mythical archaism . . . that was supposed to cure modernity of its ills' and a 'place of immutable order that contrasted with the chaotic movement of modernity and history in general' (M. Pezzella, private communication). It thus became the framework for a new order in the future and for a self-assured and authoritarian rhetoric and grandiloquence in the present. Its task was not to revisit the 'classical' as such, but to put it forward in an updated form to compete with modernism, assert the oneness of the present with that mythical past, and project it into a future that would be as immutable and mythical as the past. It was thus entirely consistent that the buildings Albert Speer designed for his Führer were not only conceived for a 'thousand-year' regime, but also for their future *Ruinenwert*, their 'value as ruins' which they would take on at the end of time.

This vision of the 'classical', which some scholars of ancient history and art found attractive (either because of their sympathies for totalitarian ideologies, or because it was another welcome legitimization of their profession), was opposed by other scholars who continued to look for diversity rather than uniformity in 'classical' cultures. So at the opposite extreme, there emerged the figure of Aby Warburg (1866–1929), a cultural historian who developed his own vision of the 'classical', one that was fairly marginal at the time but would later prove to be remarkably productive. It is extremely significant that Warburg reflected on the nature of the 'classical' not as a classicist but because of his own passionate desire to understand the nature of the Renaissance, which was the principal object of his studies. In relation to the Renaissance, the 'classical' appeared to be a powerful but remote cultural framework. He felt that the centrality of this rebirth at the very heart of European history demanded a more profound explanation: 'our resolve to examine a question that engrosses us (which in my case is the influence of the ancients) demands that we enter terrain that is as yet unexplored'. This meant he could not only look to the 'classical' age and the Renaissance, but had to search for conceptual tools to explain 'rebirth' in terms of cultural history. He wanted to know how that depository of cultural memory (the 'classical') was able to seal itself shut like a sepulchre and then open to release new life, and how every new incarnation could vary profoundly through a dynamic process intimately wound up with historical development. He wanted to know how the basic features of the 'classical' kept mutating and yet every time its fine balance between death and new life was reasserted to confirm this unceasing cycle.

Warburg perceived what he called in the language of his time *Nachleben der Antike* (survival of the ancient) – the reappearance of iconographic formulas and cultural associations sometimes centuries after they had appeared entirely defunct – as the central drama of the European cultural memory, ceaselessly threatened by the ultimate barbarity of oblivion (destruction). He focused on a process by which iconographic schemata and expressive formulas (he called these *Pathosformeln*) revive after centuries not only because of their own vitality, but also because the artist's eye 'recognizes' them. It could be described as a highly dramatic alternation between loss of meaning (in correspondence with the increasing inflexibility of dying formulas) and the reacquisition of meaning (in correspondence with the reactivation of the same formulas). Examples are the gesture of desperation and the expressive power of lifelessness mentioned in chapter 10. These were invented in the 'classical' age and following many long centuries of oblivion, the former was resurrected by Nicola Pisano and Giotto, and the latter by Raphael. In Warburg's opinion, this sudden appropriation of an ancient artistic heritage (in this case during the Florentine Renaissance) can only be explained by a process based on sympathy, an act of *Einfühlung* (entering another's mindset) that makes it possible to rediscover the meaning (and the related aesthetic emotions) behind the rigidity of the formula that has fallen into disuse.

Warburg adopted the epistemological model used by his teacher in Bonn, the classicist Hermann Usener (1834–1905), in his *Götternamen* (1896), and elevated it to the status of interpretative key for European cultural history. Usener maintained that the name of every god contains within itself something of its 'divine essence', and therefore explains both the god's ethos and the origin of the cult. It was also supposed to throw light on the spirit of the men who created each god by naming him and associating him with the passions, fears and desires from which his essence was drawn. The *nomen divinum* has a root, and in that root the original impetus that led to the god being created can still be felt. According to Warburg's *Kulturwissenschaft* (the science and study of culture), the expressive formulas created by the ancients have an innermost creative nucleus whose power remains intact under its shrivelled husk, even if for centuries no one gave a thought to such formulas on forgotten sarcophagi and other works in relief. If, on the other hand, they were handed down and repeated unthinkingly, there was little or no understanding of their power and expressive potential. But precisely because of their hidden but fervent expressive core, sooner or later an artist would 'recognize' these formulas, resurrect them and put them back into circulation (hence the rebirth). It could be said, not only in the metaphorical sense, that the artist who perceives the potential of an ancient iconographical element, adopts it and restores its ancient forcefulness and power, is moved by a kind of etymological zeal. This process could be replicated in academic research when historians are capable of going through it in its entirety with the tools of philology and, one might say, 'tabulating it', as Warburg did in his unfinished atlas, *Mnemosyne*. This staggering synopsis of the West's cultural memory maps, espouses and revives the itineraries of the mind and of culture in a dazzling combination of images.

The radical question of why apparently devitalized elements of past cultures can suddenly be reactivated (or reborn) required not only the historical tools (philology, linguistics, history of art, etc.) used to analyse Graeco-Roman or European civilization, but also a much wider comparative study of other cultures. Thus Usener and later Warburg resorted to comparing Greeks and Romans to other peoples (particularly ones with 'primitive' customs) and the European Renaissance with other 'renaissances'. This proved to be an important step. Usener wanted to test out the *Götternamen* not only on Apollo and Zeus, but also on ancient German, Lithuanian and Latvian gods. Warburg studied a local 'renaissance of antiquity' amongst the Hopi of Arizona, which was taking place at the time. A potter of great talent, Nampeyo, had just reintroduced themes and motifs dating back five centuries into the decorative ceramic repertoire of the village of Hano, and these themes and motifs had been discovered through archaeological digs. Warburg had another precedent in mind – that of Burckhardt who, in his desire to understand the essence and root of the Italian Renaissance, wondered 'whether there aren't important historical parallels; in short, other renaissances', and sought them out amongst the Jews following the exile and in Sassanian Persia. Warburg decided that this paradigm had to be verified in the field, and he therefore adopted the anthropological approach, which was to lead him to his study of the Hopi whose Native American renaissance he had come across by chance.

For both Warburg and Usener, the comparative study of cultures was required by the radical nature of the question they were trying to resolve. Warburg's project in particular needed to explain man's response to images from the

contemporary world too – indeed, above all from the contemporary world. This explanation had to be found without
reference to the status of art in contemporary society and
therefore of 'artistic-ness' as a value. In the aesthetic response
of modern man, he perceived the remote and innermost kernel of human nature, something that was therefore identical
to primitive man's reactions to images (and to the world).
During the most ancient periods of human history, this
nucleus of warmth and passion turned images into one of
the instruments for helping man to find his direction in the
world and for his laborious search for harmony through control of the other-than-self, which continued in what we might
call a phylogenetical manner up until the present, albeit in a
profoundly modified form. Warburg considered the expressive value of such images and the cyclical mechanism by
which they die and are reborn to be a continuous thread
leading back through time, which could be followed in order
to understand both the expressive formulas capable of pro-
voking aesthetic emotion and the manner in which they
periodically crumble into nothing – in other words, the dramatic alternation between memory and oblivion, a constant
threat. Thus Warburg believed that the study of the Renaissance, or rather *renaissances* (in Europe and elsewhere),
involved studying the life cycles of forms (forever leading an
unstable existence between death and rebirth) in order to
understand what we have come to know as 'art' in the last
two centuries.

However Warburg, the disciple of Usener, also had to
measure up to the prevailing concept of the 'classical' as the
cornerstone of elite education, particularly in contemporary
Germany, as well as the classicist tradition typified by Wilam-
owitz, the eminent philologist who was unable to conceal his
irritation with Usener's comparative approach. We can illus-
trate the manner in which Warburg's attitudes evolved by
comparing two references to the same passage from Goethe's
Faust which were separated by four years and contained significant differences. On the first occasion, he used the quote
as an epigraph to his essay on prophecies of pagan-Hellenistic

origin during the age of Luther (1920), and Goethe's words (*Faust*, II, lines 7742–3) were transcribed exactly:

> *Es ist ein altes Buch zu blättern:*
> *Vom Harz bis Hellas immer Vettern!*

> (It is an old book to be leafed through:
> from Harz to Greece, always kinsfolk!)

In *Faust* these lines are spoken by Mephistopheles in the Walpurgis Night episode: Mephistopheles talks to the Lamias (who were a cross between figures from classical mythology and medieval witches), and then to Empusa, who had been taken from Hecate's retinue. She addresses him as *Vetter* (cousin), and he replies sarcastically that it is an old story – witches and devils can be found everywhere and they all resemble each other. However, Warburg puts these words to an entirely different use – that of a 'kinship' between Germany (represented by the Harz mountain range) and Greece, and a continuum between ancient pagan superstitions and prophecies at the time of Luther. With his typical wit, Warburg both confirmed and ridiculed the assimilation of Germany to ancient Greece by referring to the original Goethian context and by shifting the Greece-Germany affinity from the context of 'classical' education (something that had become almost obligatory) to that of popular superstition.

The scene is somewhat different four years later at the famous lecture on the Hopi snake ritual (1923, not published until 1939) when the epigraph became:

> *Es ist ein altes Buch zu blättern:*
> *Athen-Oraibi, alles Vettern.*

> (It is an old book to be leafed through:
> Athens-Oraibi, all kinsfolk.)

This wording clearly presupposes not only Goethe's lines but also the use Warburg himself put them to in his study of the Lutheran age. Germany and the exclamation mark have disappeared along with every trace of irony. Athens stands for

Greece, and the Hopi village of Oraibi (which Warburg visited) for all the Pueblos. Athens moves into first place for metrical reasons, but possibly for other reasons too. As in the whole of this essay on the snake ritual, the affinity between modern Germany and ancient Greece has given way to the affinity between ancient Greece and another paganism – the Native American one. The intercultural (or metacultural) kinship referred to here clearly asserts the principle of comparability between cultures that have no historical relationship. This is a parallel between two similar historical evolutions (two renaissances) that cannot be explained in terms of cultural influence, and must therefore imply a more profound mechanism relating to human nature.

The dates spanned by the lives of Usener and Warburg demonstrate the long pedigree of the need to study 'classical' culture on the basis of its otherness, and not of its identity with our own. The intuitive realization that comparison with 'other' cultures could help our understanding of the 'classical' has an even longer pedigree, and goes back at least to the eighteenth century, but the further we go back in tracing its roots, the more we realize how far we are from resolving the question. In spite of these precedents, the task of understanding the 'classical' by this route is still unfinished and highly topical. In the first place, this means relativizing the oneness of the 'classical' by acknowledging its inner fault-lines and many regional variants. In the second place but of no less importance, this means highlighting the extent of the contacts between the classical and 'others' and of its debt to them, as is revealed by each of those variants. Thus the decision to treat the 'classical' as comparable with other cultures means profoundly undermining and ultimately destroying that rounded a-historical classicism on which so many arguments and projects concerning history and modern culture appear to be firmly based. This is perhaps the only way to restore value to the products of 'classical' cultures from Homer to Constantine, and this renewed value cannot be founded on an immutable model that transcends history (such a thing would be unthinkable). No, it would have to become a perpetual benchmark whose presence cannot be ignored because of its relentless cyclical return and its part within the theatre of comparison between our culture and the cultures of other peoples. History and 'classical' civilizations can thus become an 'elsewhere' that extends over space and time, another land in which to travel, occasionally recognizing something familiar but more often marvelling at the unexpected and the surprising. They can enter a broader and more refreshing landscape that, given the presence of the 'other' cultures with which they came into contact, now includes all the constituent elements of our modern world. Precisely because it has always been considered a model, the 'classical' has the potential to become the quintessential history and memory of the 'other'. Because of the inherent difficulties in understanding that otherness and avoiding the temptation to reduce it to something identical to ourselves, this task can force us to experience the joy of discovery and rediscovery, and to apply a rigorous intellectual discipline using the well-established instruments of the science of antiquity (without which the authenticity of our discoveries could not be guaranteed).

15   Cyclical Histories

If we want to understand the 'classical', we need to reject both the idea that the Western cultural tradition is closed and definitively settled as a result of its unique and unrepeatable peculiarities (which are however rarely explained), and the opposing idea that the Western cultural tradition does not exist as such (or cannot be described as a distinct entity, which amounts to the same thing). The first of these concepts can easily be translated into a preconceived 'superiority' of the West, whose power ultimately arises not from its cultural characteristics but its pre-eminence on the political and military stage over the last few centuries and to this day. The second, which is often simply a reaction against the excesses of the first, risks reducing highly complex cultural processes to a meaningless simplification by fragmenting cultures of the Western tradition at will and renouncing the task of trying to understand their meaning and significance.

It can be argued that, even though the Western cultural tradition has been signally permeated by many other cultural traditions without which it cannot be fully understood (such as Islamic or Indian ones), it does at least have one distinctive characteristic: precisely this continuous cycle of 'deaths' and 'rebirths' which Ernst Howald has called the 'rhythmical form' of European cultural history (see chapter 13). It has therefore developed its own particular posture and above all a sensitivity towards ruins; this model of cultural history needs ruins of the past around which to build and link fragments of memory (what J. B. Jackson has called the 'necessity for ruins'). In this, it differs from other civilizations dominated by a sense of continuity, as in the case of China, Japan, India and indeed Islam, which believes in an absolute continuity from the Hegira to the present day. And thus it could be argued that continuity tends to result in forms and levels of oblivion, whereas the perception of discontinuity (rifts or traumas) tends to reinforce the surviving authority of the ancient, create a nucleus of memory and increase the efficacy of ancient models precisely because they are ancient. In other words, it could be said that awareness of the time gap is a powerful incentive for creative reinvention, which on each occasion makes use of discrete elements 'fished' out of the past and chosen as a paradigm.

It has to be asked to what degree the 'rhythmical form' is peculiar to the West. Is it really true that comparison with other cultures does not reveal something similar? There are several possible responses to this question. For example, there is a widely held idea among Amerindian cultures that present-day humanity and indeed the whole world is the result of a series of catastrophes, each of which was followed by a new creative act. Hopi mythology is still alive, along with 'pagan' forms of worship, and according to Hopi cosmogony, today's world is the Fourth World and the product of the destruction of the first three.

> The First World was *Tokpela* ('the Infinite Space'), which was created by the sole original God, Taiowa. Taiowa created the Nephew-God, Sótuknang, who in turn created the waters, the air, the earth and then Kókyangwúti, the Spider-Woman, who in turn created the Twins, Pöqáng-hoya and Palöngaw-hoya. They ordered the world, and then Taiowa gave them the task of creating humanity: the First People lived happily and harmoniously with each other and with the animals until Lavaíhoya ('He Who Speaks') arrived in the form of a bird. He persuaded them

of the difference between men and animals, and between different types of men, while also convincing them not to revere Taiowa. Then came the Serpent Káto'ya, who increased discord. The Nephew-God, Sótuknang, then spoke to Taiowa, and together they decided that this world needed to be destroyed, and only a few were worthy of being saved. They were closed up in a cave, where the people of the Ants lived, and the world was destroyed by enormous eruptions of all the volcanoes of the earth.

Once the earth had cooled down, the Second World was created and its name was *Tokpa* ('Dark Midnight'). The Nephew-God, Sótuknang, put land where previously there had been sea, and vice versa, and at last allowed the Second People to emerge from their caves (the First Emergence). But after a passage of time, men started to become increasingly covetous and eventually they ceased praying to the Creator. Then came the Nephew-God, Sótuknang, who destroyed this world too, and saved the few who still prayed to the gods, in the caves of the Ants. The Second World was destroyed by ice.

The Third World, which was called *Kuskurza* ('Lost in Time'), was created once the earth had warmed up again, and men could leave the lairs of the Ants (the Second Emergence). The men of this Third People then created great cities in which they lived together, but soon they became too absorbed in their own affairs and ceased to sing the praises of the Creator. Indeed, they started to make war against each other, and Taiowa decided to punish them with another destruction. The few who still sang the praises of the Creator were led into an area protected by tall plants with hollow trunks, and the Nephew-God, Sótuknang, destroyed the word by water (a kind of biblical deluge).

Once the waters had receded, there was the Third Emergence, and from the hollow trees in which they sheltered emerged the Fourth People who immediately set out in search of the Fourth World under the leadership of the Spider-Woman. They found it after a long search, and it was called *Túwakachi* ('Complete World'): this is the world in which we live.

Similar versions of this cosmogonic myth can be found in other Amerindian civilizations. Indeed the mythopoeic power associated with it must still be alive, given that in 1996 a Sioux priest proclaimed the imminent end of the Fourth World and the beginning of the Fifth (Nelson 2000).

The case of the Hopi is not an isolated one. Even in cultures closer to ours, it is not difficult to find the image of a cultural history of humanity (or of a people) founded on a sequence of catastrophes separated by an equal number of rebirths. Across the world in India, the Vedantic texts put forward a cyclical vision of the cosmos, which passes through an infinite number of creations and destructions. The Bible also tells of two dramatic rifts in the history of mankind: the Expulsion from Eden (which in Hopi terms could be described as the end of the First World) and Noah's Flood (which in Hopi terms could be described as the end of the Second World). In Ireland, a tradition contained in the *Lebar Gabála* ('Book of Settlements', eleventh century) explains the settlement of the island as a series of invasions (the first from Spain), each of which ends with the death of all the invaders, with the exception of the last ones, from which all the Irish descend. An important variant is to be found in *Scél Tuáin Meic Chairill* ('The Story of Tuán, Son of Cairell', ninth century), according to which the protagonist, Tuán, belonged to the first wave of settlement in Ireland, but survived all the subsequent phases of settlement and resettlement by transforming himself on each occasion into a different animal. In the end he returns to his human form, retains his memory of the cyclical sequence of events and is therefore capable of narrating them (Carey 1994).

These stories cannot fail to remind us of the succession of Hesiodic peoples or even the *palaioi logoi* (ancient stories) to which Plato refers in Book Three of his *Laws*. Let us examine the latter example more closely. In the dialogue between an Athenian and a Cretan called Cleinias (676 A and ff), the

initial theme (the origins of the *politeia* or forms of government) turns into a discussion on changes in the forms of
government over time as thousands of *poleis* come into
being and equal numbers are destroyed: gradually 'small
states have become bigger, and big ones have grown smaller;
superior states have deteriorated and bad ones have
improved'. This continuous change in human affairs was
nothing more, if the 'ancient stories' are to be believed, than
a reflection of the general mutability of the world. It was
told that 'the human race has been repeatedly annihilated
by floods and plagues and many other causes, so that only a
small fraction of it survived', and moreover they are 'quite
innocent of . . . crafty devices'. Thus every catastrophe has to
be followed by another arduous process of civilization(Sassi
1986; Cambiano 2002).

   Similarly in Plato's *Timaeus* (22 B and ff), an Egyptian
priest says to Solon, 'you Greeks are all children, and a Greek
is never old,' and then goes on to explain, 'you do not have
any ancient tradition . . . There have been many catastrophes
for humanity in the past, and there will be many more in the
future, the majority of which are due to fire and water, but
other minor ones have various other causes.' When the catastrophe is caused by heavenly fire, people living close to the
sea (or the Nile) can save themselves, and when it is caused
by floods and deluges, the people living in the mountains are
the ones to be saved. On each occasion, according to the
Egyptian, something of man's traditions and knowledge is
saved but most is lost, and while the Egyptians retain some
memory of this alternation between catastrophes and newly
founded civilizations, in the case of the Greeks 'on each occasion only the illiterate manage to save themselves, and they
have to start from the very beginning without any memory of
the ancient times' (fortunately the Egyptians even retained a
memory of Greek events).

   This very restricted sample suggests that both cosmogony
and the cultural history of humanity (or a particular civilization) was represented as a succession of catastrophes and
'rebirths' (or new 'emergences') not only by the cultural

traditions used here as examples but in many others besides. If then this narrative paradigm is so widely used, what is supposed to be so distinctive about the Western cultural tradition? What is 'original' or 'unique' in this succession of 'deaths' and 'rebirths' of the ancient that constitute Howald's 'rhythmical form'? And to what extent is the role of the 'classical' in the European cultural tradition subsequently modified?

In spite of appearances, this comparative background adds to the uniqueness of the Western tradition. While it is true that a sequence of catastrophes and new beginnings is a common theme for Hopis, Indians and Greeks in the creation of a mythical period and the resulting narratives, it is no less true that in the Western tradition (and probably only in that tradition) historical time is grafted onto mythical time, and indeed replaces it. The universal model of catastrophes projected onto a remote and elusive 'beforehand' is replaced by a sequence of actual deaths and rebirths (the end of the Roman Empire, the series of renaissances from the Carolingian one to the Renaissance proper), which can be dated and documented through historical study and can be embodied in tangible ruins. Indeed such ruins can be studied, reconstructed, restored to an at least partial or virtual wholeness that reduces but does not eliminate the effects of the catastrophe that destroyed them. The mythical model of catastrophes was able to become an historical reality and the object of historical study, as the result of very particular and unrepeatable historical circumstances (that balance between 'excessive continuity' and 'excessive discontinuity' which I attempted to define by contrasting examples in chapter 13).

This has always been a distinguishing feature of the Western cultural tradition in its 'power relations' with other cultures. Carlo Ginzburg wrote in a wonderful essay on this point, 'Dialogue between cultures, cultural multiplicity: the example examined here [the *Démoiselles d'Avignon*] reminds us of an often forgotten truism, namely that not all cultures command the same power.' According to Ginzburg, the power of the Western figurative tradition (in which Picasso grew up) consists of an enormous 'real and potential capacity for inclusiveness', and thus Picasso 'managed to decipher the codes of African images' by juxtaposing them with recognizable echoes of classical art. In practice, this capacity was inseparable from 'the power of a cultural tradition that had provided the ideological justifications and intellectual tools for the European conquest of the world'. We have to ask ourselves to what extent the assimilation of mythical time into historical time contributed to the construction of a model for cultural history (or at least, for the representation of our *own* cultural history) in terms of continuous, repeated and cyclical deaths and rebirths. Can we say that the 'capacity for inclusiveness' of elements taken from other cultures presupposes the cyclical return to the 'classical', and is indeed superimposed on it? It could be argued that it is the periodic return to that 'other-than-self' called the 'Ancient' that generates the search for and cultural inclusion of a different 'other-than-self' in the distant cultures of China, Japan and Africa.

Even though history has a cyclical and recursive movement, it should be observed that 'every time the returns are similar but also different, because they are modified by the new situations in which they occur. Each return cycle takes place on a different level' and therefore 'the image that illustrates this cyclical trajectory is not the circle but rather the spiral. The rebirths, even when they manifest common or similar elements, are original and different experiences on each occasion: indeed it is principally the differences that produce meaning' (unpublished article by G. B. Conte). On every rebirth (new beginning or 'cultural phase'), this evolutionary model specifically and innately seeks out models primarily taken from Graeco-Roman antiquity but also from other cultures *for the purpose of inclusion* (see chapter 16). As the spiral of cyclical returns coils its way through history, the 'classical' is reclassified into new roles and recurring roles. On the one hand, this ongoing process of de-signification and re-signification constitutes the story-line of European cultural history and, on the other, it is itself the object of our historical investigation.

Claude Lévi-Strauss's distinction between 'hot' societies and 'cold' societies is well known (see Charbonnier 1959). 'Cold' societies are not outside history (like Ranke's *Völker ohne Geschichte* [peoples without history]), and their past is as ancient as ours. However, 'throughout history, these societies seem to have developed a particular wisdom which makes them fiercely resist any change to their structure that would allow history to break through their defences'. For Lévi-Strauss, this 'coldness' is not of course a shortcoming or deficiency, but rather the product of a cultural evolution and a 'particular wisdom'. 'Cold' societies persist in their nature through myth and ritual, whereas 'hot' societies generate change through technological development and cultural memory. In his important work on cultural memory, Jan Assmann (2001) put forward another interpretative model which denies the distinction between 'hot societies' and 'cold societies'. According to Assmann, different cultures develop different strategies for the management of cultural memory and different uses of the past, which necessarily contain elements that relate to one or other pole. Societies therefore define themselves not in terms of being entirely 'hot' or entirely 'cold' (as Lévi-Strauss had already admitted), but rather in the manner in which each mixes generators of 'coldness' and generators of 'heat' in their own particular manner and in constantly new combinations. He argued that the ancient Egyptian culture and the ancient Mesopotamian cultures produced two opposing strategies for managing historical memory: the Egyptian king guaranteed the cyclical repetition of time and was therefore the principal agent of anti-history, whereas history was at the command of the Mesopotamian sovereign, who needed it to give his regime legitimacy. It is this latter tradition that influenced both biblical historiography and the Greek historical tradition (the Egyptian's tale in *Timaeus* also lends itself to being interpreted in the light of this distinction, but it shifts the Egyptians to the 'hot' category, given that they retain historical memory unlike the Greeks).

Against the background of these vast historical-interpretative perspectives, it can be argued that the assimilation (or enactment) of the mythical and cyclical time of catastrophes (a 'cold' element) within the historical (and therefore 'hot') cycle of deaths and rebirths of the ancient, with its cumbersome trail of ruins, is a peculiarity of the European cultural tradition and indeed its particular strongpoint.

16   The Future of the 'Classical'

As we have seen, the 'classical' is presented in each of its various incarnations as a *postulate* more or less to be taken for granted, but in reality it always reflects a *project*, and therefore can serve as a litmus test for understanding its features and implications on a case by case basis. For instance, the unresolved 'dualism' of Roman art (examined in chapter 7) reflects the historiographical differences between a Middle Age that was distant from 'classical' arts and their rebirth. The ancient was a mixture of Greek and Roman with a predominance of the Roman for Vasari and other Italians, whereas for Winckelmann the Greeks played a similar role to Raphael and Michelangelo, and the Romans were shifted into the same category as medieval art. Onto this was then grafted the Viennese *fin-de-siècle* re-evaluation of Roman art (Wickhoff and Riegl), which was entirely absorbed with its *afterwards*, with European medieval art (see chapter 7). It was the relationship between Roman art and the 'classical' that caused the former to fulfil two opposing roles: that of the basis and foundation for the development of medieval art, and curiously that of the principal source of models and norms for the Renaissance – the visible remains of the underlying reality of an undivided 'classicism' initially seen as indistinguishably Graeco-Roman, but from which it was then possible gradually to separate out Greek art and eventually to contrast it with the Roman.

As this example clearly demonstrates, the sudden changes and contradictions in the extent, definition and use of the 'classical' (of which I have only cited a few examples) never challenge its existence, although they might challenge its identity or identification. Far from weakening Howald's analysis that the rebirth of the 'classical' takes on a 'rhythmical form' in European cultural history, these fertile shifts in the interpretation of the 'classical' actually strengthen it (see chapter 13). If it is possible to put the 'classical' to so many different and indeed contradictory uses that continuously change its image, then this is primarily because we continue in spite of everything to associate the 'classical' with values we consider universal, such as perfection, balance, grace, intensity and naturalness of expression. These values have been attributed (on the whole implicitly) to the 'classical' since antiquity itself and then by a long tradition of messages that are always contemporary and concern the fullness of civilization, which project these values as timeless and perpetual and claim that they are not historically determined.

However, this presumed perennial topicality – particularly of the Greek 'classical' – is not simply the product of the way it has been used and abused. Quite the opposite, it is often taken as a given, and implicitly considered 'pre-ideological' (in spite of all the evidence to the contrary). Thus Karl Marx wrote in *Grundrisse* in 1857:

> In the case of the arts, it is well known that certain periods in the flowering are out of all proportion to the general development of society, hence also to the material foundation, the skeletal structure as it were, of its organization. For example, the Greeks compared to the moderns or also Shakespeare ... But the difficulty lies not in understanding that the Greek arts and epic are bound up with certain forms of social development. The difficulty is that they can still afford artistic pleasure and that in a certain

respect they count as a norm and as an unattainable model.

The apparent paradox, as previously noted, is that the supposed timelessness of 'classical', particularly 'classical' Greek civilization and art, becomes all the stronger the more we ignore the historical process that determined the forms and myriad features of the 'classical' and could relate it to other phenomena, for by so doing we restrict its significance. In the name of this much-vaunted immutable and paradigmatic nature of the 'classical', Graeco-Roman antiquity has ended up being identified with the common root of the civilization we came to know as the 'West', precisely in the sense of Hegel's claim, 'On hearing the name "Greece", a cultured European man immediately feels himself to be in his home country'. The 'classical' appears here as the very *foundation* of Western culture and history. And it is supposed to have given rise not only to results, actions and memories, but also to values that are still relevant. Contemporary values can then be legitimized by declaring them identical or close to the 'classical' ones (the less explicitly this is done, the more effective it is).

This concept, which assumes the 'classical' to be a founding value and one that goes beyond the national, is primarily a faded legacy of the high status of 'classical' education up until quite recently. It is, however, typical of our times that this concept can maintain and indeed consolidate its position while the place of the 'classical' in education systems and our widely shared culture is fast disappearing. In this context, it becomes much easier to perpetuate the stereotype of 'classicism' as the cradle and endorsement of the West and to use it with impunity, given that this trend drastically reduces the number of citizens capable of challenging it knowledgeably. Like every other image of the 'classical', this stereotype appears in the guise of a postulate, but actually reflects a project: that of constructing a solid and unassailable identity for the West, which encompasses not only Dante, Shakespeare, Corneille, Goethe, Leonardo da Vinci and

Rembrandt, but also and above all the Graeco-Roman 'classical' age, because it is the shared substratum that no Western nation can claim as exclusively or prevalently its own.

This image of the 'classical' is thus bound up with the concept of a West with clear and sealed frontiers, typified by extreme dynamism and contrasting with the eternally static East. It is not only determinedly Eurocentric; it also exactly overlaps the concept of Western civilization as superior to every other one, and therefore legitimizes colonialism's expansionist or hegemonic policies and economic and cultural subjugation. The opposition between Greeks and barbarians is then translated into the one between the West and the others, now given new life and projected onto Asia and Africa. It can be reasonably argued that this *reductio ad unum* of the complexity of ancient cultures is destined to have devastating results, because it tends to trivialize 'classical' culture and empty it of all meaning at exactly the same time in which its superiority is declared. It risks embalming it and turning it into a lifeless icon just as it is destined increasingly to become the dominion of a few specialists and to disappear from citizens' cultural horizon. The tiresome preaching of those who advocate a rebirth of 'classical' education in the name of its eternal and ideal values is an irrelevant product of this great cultural shift that marginalizes the 'classical' and at the same time turns it into an icon.

There is nothing new about this contrast between the idea of a timeless and immutable 'classicism' (which is widely held in popular culture and political rhetoric) and the assiduous work of specialists who know and explore the inner contradictions and features of the 'classical', as well as its debts to 'other' cultures. It perpetuates the rift between the two opposing images of the 'classical' which have already been mentioned (see chapter 14), and indeed one of these – the supposed timelessness of the 'classical' – lent itself during the interwar period to manipulation by totalitarian regimes that appropriated, twisted and further simplified it, so that it could be used as an instrument for self-promotion and attainment of legitimacy. Even in our own times, it is possible to choose between two opposing uses of the 'classical', the one that turns it into an icon and a rigid set of values, and the one that seeks out its variety and its complexity as an historical experience. The first and most frequent use of the 'classical' happily accepts and indeed encourages the ongoing decline of classical studies in educational curricula (icons are revered, not studied); conversely the second use demands that we question the meaning and future of the 'classical' in schools, universities and the culture shared by citizens.

The continuing dominant use of the former would thwart any ideas on the future of the 'classical' and classical studies. However there is a very attractive alternative to that image of the 'classical' as something perpetual, unchanging and identical to ourselves – that 'belongs to the West' and only to the West. In his briefest of essays ('Les trois humanismes', 1956), Claude Lévi-Strauss suggested that the rediscovery of 'classical' antiquity in the Renaissance can be seen as 'an early form of ethnology', given that they then 'understood that no civilization can think about itself, if it does not have other societies with which to compare itself': the renewed presence of the ancient thus introduced 'the technique of defamiliarization' as an intellectual exercise, and triggered a cultural revolution with a tremendous reach, whose consequences are still with us – indeed they have not yet fully made themselves felt. According to Lévi-Strauss, the appearance of ethnology was nothing less than a prolongation of the first humanism: the study of the Ancients (an 'elsewhere' in time rather than space) naturally evolved into the study of civilizations outside Europe (an 'elsewhere' in space rather than in time). Of Lévi-Strauss's three humanisms, the first had Graeco-Roman antiquity as its object of study (or of defamiliarization), the second the great oriental civilizations (such as India, China and Japan), and the third the cultures once called 'primitive' – those 'without history' of the *Naturvölker* (peoples in the state of nature).

In a stunning historical résumé, Lévi Strauss asks us to re-examine the study and emulation of the Ancients and treat it as a form of latent anthropology. His interpretative model

hinges on the Renaissance or rebirth of antiquity, and therefore incorporates the perennial theme of the 'classical' that
dies and returns to life: in other words, it is another version –
an anthropological version – of Howald's analysis of the
recurring rebirth of the 'classical' as a 'rhythmical form' of
European cultural history. In Lévi-Strauss's version, however,
the rediscovery of the (Graeco-Roman) 'classical' is not associated with a stable system of Western values to be contrasted
with those of 'others'; quite the contrary, it is inserted in a
series of discoveries of 'other' cultures in a crescendo that
starts with the 'classical' but needs to expand to all civilizations. According to this interpretation, the distinguishing
feature of the Western cultural tradition is the transition
from the study of the classics as a technique for defamiliarization to the study (by its very nature 'inclusive' – see
chapter 15) of 'other' civilizations and therefore anthropology. Because it returns generation after generation with a
mixture of similarities and diversities, the 'classical' is
increasingly bound with elements taken from *other* cultural
traditions. Every time new meanings are given to the 'classical', it is revitalized by its increasing 'inclusiveness', and this
will continue in the future.

Viewed in this manner, the two poles of identity and
otherness, to which I have given such emphasis, are dramatically repositioned: they can now coexist, because both are
possible (and will be even more so in the future) whether
we are thinking of the Greeks, the Chinese, the Mayans or
the African Ife civilization. Arnaldo Momigliano's question,
which was posed at the very beginning of this book,
can now meet with a new response: it is worth studying
Graeco-Roman 'classical' culture because of the manner in
which it continuously shifts between identity and otherness,
and in which it feels like 'ours' even though we acknowledge
its 'diversity' from us. It is worth studying because it is in-
trinsic to Western culture and indispensable if we want to
understand Western culture, but also because it encourages
us to study and understand 'other' cultures. It is worth
studying because it is a depository of values which we can

still recognize as õur own, but also because of what is irredeemably alien about those values.

If this is true, then a revival of classical studies within a 'global' context should go further than simply challenging the stale mainstream image of the 'classical' as a timeless value, and put forward a vision of the 'classical' for the future. This would mean developing a few inspirational principles for the new status of classical studies in a cultural context which is now experiencing radical change. To achieve this we need a unitary concept of the 'sciences of antiquity', and must therefore challenge the excessive fragmentation of classical disciplines – a fragmentation of aims and intentions that often prevents us from acknowledging the progressive marginalization of classical studies in the modern world, not to mention devising a new plan and role for the 'classical'. If we are to embark on creating such a plan, then we can start by pointing out the three principal directions in which we must move, none of which is autonomous – indeed they are all highly interdependent.

Firstly, the 'classical' must be considered the 'departure point' for modern Europe's vernacular cultures, but with complete awareness of its repeated deaths and rebirths, and its essential role of providing European cultural history with its characteristic and unique 'rhythmical form'.

Secondly, the Graeco-Roman 'classical' age could be seen as a gigantic experiment in economic and cultural globalization whose zenith was reached in the middle centuries of the Roman Empire. We have the advantage of knowing about its formation and the timing and causes of its final collapse. The comparison – now particularly topical in the United States – between the Roman Empire and the American one demonstrates how pressing is the need to discover precedents and explore parallels not only in imperialist rhetoric but also in the anxieties over the crisis and disintegration of 'complex societies' of yesterday and today (Tainter 1988). The cultural history of the 'classical' age could be the ideal place for analysing and comparing cultures (again with particular reference to the present day), both because it lends itself to the exploration of mutual borrowing between ancient cultures such as those of Mesopotamia, Egypt and Greece, or those of Etruria, Rome, Gaul and Britannia, and because that ancient cultural exchange is itself of great interest to us, because European cultures were born from it and not from some immaculate and exclusively Graeco-Roman 'classicism'. That exchange between cultures made us what we are today.

Thirdly, the 'classical' can and must be the key for accessing an even wider comparison with 'other' cultures in a genuinely 'global' manner. This is not only for the reasons put forward by Lévi-Strauss. For example, other cultures besides the Western one are rich in texts, images and thought that relate to 'classical' civilization (this is the case with Arab philosophy and science, or with Indian art and mathematics). Moreover, now that we live in a 'global' context we need to explore all cultures across the millennia, and pay particular attention to the timing of cultural formation and interchange (hence the 'classical' age as one amongst others). The forms of cultural hegemony, cultural assimilation and 'globalization' in the Graeco-Roman world could be a good model against which to gauge and better understand similar processes in the contemporary world, even though these are occurring on a much larger scale. Evoking the other-than-self that is within us (the 'classical') could then be an essential step closer to an understanding of otherness outside ourselves (other cultures), if we can repeat Rimbaud's words from a letter of 1871 and fully understand them: '*Je* est un autre'.

Finally, it should also be said that those who would like to deny or destroy any ongoing presence of the 'classical' in the modern world should at least know something more about it if they wish to avoid being caught up in it unawares. An example cited by Llewellyn Morgan in 2003 shows how this can happen. The Latin poet Lucilius (second century BC) wrote that the Roman people were 'often defeated in a battle but never in a war' (*praelio victus, non bello*). Although his work was lost, this quotation, which is known to us through Nonius Marcellus (fourth century AD), was popularized during the Renaissance by Erasmus, and became a widely used *topos*. Indeed it became so widely used that today it has on several occasions been employed polemically against Western culture. Thus a Vietnamese document argued that 'Vietnam has lost many battles, but never a war'. According to the Party of Islamic Liberation (an extremist group that demands the re-establishment of the caliphate), 'Islam has lost a few battles, but has always won the wars.' The Nigerian Dahiru Yahya, who advocates the introduction of *shariah* in his country to counter all Western influences (particularly 'Latin Christianity'), declares that during its periodic clashes with the West, Islam 'has won and lost many battles, but has never lost the war'. This invective against the West feeds on scraps and fragments of Western 'classical' culture. Those who deploy this invective are probably unaware of its origin, and thus demonstrate the extent to which a cultural tradition that is considered to be on the way out still retains a hidden vitality. This could be said of the Japanese Nausicaa or the Homeric reference from a member of the Taliban (see chapter 1), as well as the great mass of references to 'classical' texts and images that pervade Western culture. The persistent recycling of the ancient in tiny fragments entirely removed from all historical context appears to reintroduce (whether in Nigeria or Italy) a use of history as a depository of *exempla* and not in accordance with a chain of events established by historical investigation and linked to cause and effect. In this sense, Doric columns on a post-modern building, advertising shots of cars in front of a Greek temple, and David Levine's drawings of George W. Bush dressed as a Roman emperor all belong to the same cultural reality.

This development too is not without precedents: antiquity was also considered a depository of *exempla* in the Middle Ages (for example the lines of *Famous Men* displayed on public and private buildings from Padua to Siena and Rome, to instruct contemporaries with the *exemplum* of the ancients). However the enormous vitality (an ethical and political, rather than an historical one) of the 'classical' model implicit in those *exempla* was eventually to consolidate the

notion that the 'classical' was innately worthy of being
known, given that it was worthy of being quoted. In the long
run, this meant focusing attention on knowledge of Graeco-
Roman antiquity, and causing the *exemplum* to revive history
through a return to texts and surviving works of art. Then as
now, the fragmentation of the 'classical' into disjointed and
decontextualized units (suitable for quoting) destroys but
also perpetuates it.

It should be emphasized in conclusion that, even in a
'global' context, the Graeco-Roman 'classical' conserves – at
least when compared with other cultural histories – a unique
and unrepeatable peculiarity that makes knowledge of it
even more crucial to an understanding of not only the broad
sweep of history but also the constituent elements of contemporary cultures, particularly the ones in the European
tradition. If the arguments I have expounded in this book are
not disproved by other studies, the peculiarity in question is
that the rebirth of the 'classical' – its continuous reappraisal
through a dramatic repetition of deaths and resurrections –
can be considered the 'rhythmical form' of European cultural
history, of which it is both an essential and unique feature,
not because other cultures lack stories about catastrophes
and cyclical returns, but because it does not appear that elsewhere the mythical model of cyclical return has been
embodied in history and itself become the object of historical
investigation (see chapter 15). While this 'rhythmical form'
hinges on the 'classical' in its endless alternation between
deaths and rebirths, the acute nostalgia that leads to the
rebirths engenders, particularly from Petrarch onwards, a
gigantic effort to recreate *historically* that bygone age. The
mythical account of catastrophes and returns, which is to be
found in so many other cultures, is here secularized and
absorbed into the historical narrative. Precisely because of
this, it could be said that the 'rhythmical form' of history in
the Western tradition takes on a generative and initiating role
not so much for anthropology as a discipline (Lévi-Strauss's
model) as for the very idea of comparison between cultures.
It triggers curiosity in 'other' cultures, justifies that curiosity

and is in turn justified by that curiosity, as a result of the markedly 'inclusive' dynamic engendered by this relationship with the 'classical'.

Of no less importance in this process is the fact that in antiquity 'classical' culture was already an extremely hybrid creation through contacts with other cultures. It could also be argued that its unrelenting re-emergence had the effect of accentuating the composite nature of the 'classical' with every 'rebirth', and making it receptive to new influences just as it became the model and reference point for new cultural situations. Conversely it is no less true that an essential and typical feature of the 'classical' – its intrinsically hybrid nature and openness to new hybridizations – favoured and at least partially caused its repeated rebirths: the cyclical 'return of the gods' of antiquity, albeit in the debased guise imagined and repudiated by Borges rather than the immaculately Olympian one envisaged by Pound (see chapter 1). The essential cultural exchanges and mixtures that make up the 'classical' and its 'rhythmical form' of continuous rebirth in history are in reality two sides of the same coin.

In this working hypothesis, the various manifestations of the 'classical' that have been examined (and the many others left outside this study) become more significant and compelling. The 'classical' may have an entitlement to become once again the object of attention and study, and it would make perfect sense to reintroduce it – in schools as well – no longer as the static and privileged jargon of the elites, but as an effective key for accessing the multiplicity of cultures in the modern world and for the help it can give us in understanding the way in which these cultures are penetrating each other. The 'classical', no longer an inflexible model, would become what it has occasionally been in the past: the stimulus for a resolute comparison not only between ancients and moderns, but also between 'our' cultures and 'other' cultures. This comparison is always played out in relation to the present, and always with an often very bitter clash between opposing interpretations of the future as well as the past. This perpetual invocation and redefinition of the 'classical' has never been anything other than an unceasing search for our ancestors who by definition are distant from us and also by definition belong to us. Those ancestors generated us and we generate and regenerate them every time we invoke them in the present and for the present. We have to look to the 'classical' not as our dead and unmerited inheritance, but as something profoundly remarkable and *alien* that needs to be re-created every day and something that is a powerful incentive to understand 'otherness'. The more we look to it in this way, the more it will have to tell us in the future. We might be tempted to say that the 'classical' has lost many battles, but never the war.

Note on the Text

This short work returns to and develops an essay written at the invitation of Wolf-Dieter Heilmeyer for inclusion in the catalogue for the exhibition on Greek classicism held in Berlin in 2002. The essay was published in its German translation ('Das Klassizismus und das Klassische. Ein Durchgang im Rückblick' in *Die Griechische Klassik. Idee oder Wircklichkeit*, Mainz 2002, pp. 25–53). I then had an opportunity to discuss and improve upon this text at a seminar Paul Zanker and I held at the Scuola Normale Superiore in Pisa with students on our two courses. At the invitation of Daniele Del Giudice, I then gave a lecture based on the essay but with several changes in emphasis and development of the argument; the lecture took place in Venice on 4 October 2003 as part of the *Fondamenta* series. The text was published before the book version of the lecture series (with a significant misprint) under the publisher's title, 'Che fine ha fatto il classico (perché sull'Antico si rischia lo scontro di classe)' (*Il Giornale dell'Arte*, no. 226, Nov 2003, pp. 50–53), and an abridged version was published in a book edited by Franco Montanari, *Rimuovere i classici? Cultura classica e società contemporanea*, Turin 2003, pp. 5–8. This expanded version also includes ideas and passages taken from my introduction to *Noi e i Greci*, Turin 1996, pp. xxvii–xxxix (vol. I of *I Greci. Storia cultura arte societa*, 4 vols, Turin 1996–2002) and from my other works, particularly 'L'idea di Rinascimento e la "vita" dell'arte romana' in *Belfagor*, LVII, no. 6, Nov 2002, pp. 659–68, and 'Roma. Eternità delle rovine' in *Eutropia*, no. 3, 2003, pp. 133–43. The present revised edition in English includes a new chapter (chapter 15), whose first version was published as 'Palinodia e interpolazione' in *Il Ponte*, LX, 2004, nos 7–8, pp. 122–8.

I am particularly grateful to Allan Cameron for his careful translation of this book. For their assistance, information and suggestions, I would equally like to thank Gianfranco Adornato, Maurizio Bettini, Pia Brancaccio, Giuseppe Cambiano, Maria Luisa Catoni, Antonio Costa, Elizabeth Cropper, Francesco de Angelis, Paola Dematté, Fabrizio Federici, Ernesto Franco, Wolf-Dieter Heilmeyer, Wu Hung, Yoshie Kojima, Sonia Maffei, Glenn Most, Mario Pezzella, Giuseppe Pucci, Andrea Settis-Frugoni and Paul Zanker, as well as all the participants in the previously mentioned seminar at the Scuola Normale Superiore in Pisa. I would like to thank Piero de Gennaro for the information he provided me on Irish myths.

Bibliography

Obviously an exhaustive bibliography on the subjects considered in this book would be much longer than the book itself and therefore inappropriate (always supposing that one would be possible). The following is therefore an unavoidably arbitrary and incomplete selection that I have generally restricted to the works referred to in this book.

CHAPTERS 1–3

Arnaldo Momigliano gave his lecture at Erice on the study of ancient Greek and Roman history to a group of secondary-school students as part of a preparatory course for university organized by the Scuola Normale di Pisa in 1967. The current definitions of the 'classical' are still mainly based on the debate that took place in the early twentieth century. Of particular note are: G. Rodenwaldt, 'Zur begrifflichen und geschichtlichen Bedeutung des Klassischen in der bildenden Kunst' in *Zeitschrift für Ästhetik*, XI, 1916, pp. 116ff; F. Matz, 'Der Begriff des Klassischen in der antiken Kunst' in *Zeitschrift für Ästhetik*, XXIII, 1929, pp. 70ff; R. Bianchi Bandinelli, *Kunst der Antike und neuzeitliche Kritik*, Groningen 1931; W. Jäger (ed.), *Das Problem des Klassischen und die Antike. Acht Vorträge gehalten auf der Fachtagung der klassischen Altertumswissenschaft zu Naumburg*, Leipzig 1931; E. Langlotz, *Griechische Klassik*, Stuttgart 1932 (4/1956); H. Rose, *Klassik als künstlerische Denkform des Abendlandes*, Munich 1937; K. Bauch, 'Klassik, Klassizität, Klassizismus' in *Werk des Künstlers*, I,

1939–40; C. J. Burckhardt, 'Zum Begriff des Klassischen in Frankreich und in der deutschen Humanität' in *Concinnitas, Wölfflin-Festschrift*, 1944, pp. 26ff. For more recent debates, see at least: M. Ciliberto, *Il Rinascimento. Storia di un dibattito*, Florence 1975; W. Vosskamp (ed.), *Klassik im Vergleich. Normativität und Historizität antiker Klassiken*, Stuttgart 1993; A. Borbein, 'Die Klassik-Diskussion in der klassischen Archäologie' in H. Flashar (ed.), *Altertumswissenschaft in den 20er Jahren. Neue Fragen und Impulse*, Stuttgart 1995; H. Pfotenhauer and P. Sprengel (eds), *Klassik und Klassizismus*, Frankfurt 1995; H. Stenzel, 'Klassik als Klassizismus' in *Der neue Pauly*, XIV, 2000, pp. 887ff; *Die Griechische Klassik. Idee oder Wircklichkeit*, exhibition catalogue, Mainz 2002.

For the authors cited in these chapters, see: H. Miyazaki, *Nausicaa of the Valley of the Wind*, 7 vols, Portland 2004; J. Stuart Mill, review of George of Grote's *History of Greece*, in *Edinburgh Review*, 1846; J. W. von Goethe, *Maximem und Reflexionen über Literatur und Ettick, Schriften*, vol. 21, ed. M. Hecker, Weimar 2007. N. Al Sayyad and M. Castells (eds), *Muslim Europe or Euro-Islam. Politics, Culture, and Citizenship in the Age of Globalization*, Oxford 2003; J. L. Borges, *Ragnarök*, 1960; J. S. Mill, *Discussions and Dissertations*, vol. II, London 1859, p. 283; L. Gernet, *Les Grecs sans miracle*, Paris 1983.

CHAPTER 4   THE 'CLASSICAL' AS THE DIVIDING
LINE BETWEEN POST-MODERN AND MODERN

R. Venturi, D. Scott Brown and S. Izenour, *Learning from Las Vegas*, Cambridge, Mass., 1972

D. Drier, *Neo Neo-Classicism. The Uses of Tradition in Late 20th Century Art*, Annandale-on-Hudson, N.Y., 1986

C. Jenks, *Post-modernism. The New Classicism in Art and Architecture*, London 1987

G. L. Hersey, *The Lost Meaning of Classical Architecture. Speculations on Ornament from Vitruvius to Venturi*, Cambridge, Mass., 1988

R. A. M. Stern and R. Gastil, *Modern Classicism*, New York 1988

S. Connor, *Post-modernist Culture*, Oxford 1989

A. Bammer, 'Antike-Moderne Postmoderne' in *Jahreshefte des Österreichischen Archäologischen Instituts*, LIX, 1989, pp. 101ff

A. Papadakis and H. Watson (eds), *New Classicism*, London 1990

D. Hezel (ed.), *Architekten. Ricardo Bofill und Taller de Arquitectura*, Stuttgart 3/1993

P. Mainardi, *The Persistence of Classicism*, Williamstown, Mass., 1995

L. Schneider, 'Il classico nella cultura postmoderna' in S. Settis (ed.), *I Greci. Storia arte cultura società*, vol. I, *Noi e i Greci*, Turin 1996, pp. 707ff

A. Papadakis, *Classical Modern Architecture*, Paris 1997

M. Dobbe, *Querelle des anciens, des modernes et des postmodernes. Exemplarische Untersuchungen zur Medienästhetik der Malerei im Anschluss an Positionen von Nicolas Poussin und Cy Twombly*, Munich 1999

CHAPTER 5   THE 'CLASSICAL' AMONGST THE 'HISTORICAL' STYLES AND THE VICTORY OF THE DORIC

N. Pevsner, *The Romantic Movement, Historicism, and the Beginning of the Modern Movement, 1760–1914. An Outline of European Architecture*, Harmondsworth 1943

K. Dohmer, *In welchem Style sollen wir bauen? Architekturtheorie zwischen Klassizismus und Jugendstil*, Munich 1976

A. Bammer, *Architektur als Erinnerung. Archäologie und Gründerzeitarchitektur in Wien*, Vienna 1977

H. Andics, *Ringstrassenzeit. Wien 1867 bis 1887*, Vienna and Munich 1983

B. Rukschcio and R. Schachel, *Adolf Loos. Leben und Werk*, Salzburg and Vienna 1987

R. J. van Pelt and C. W. Westfall, *Architectural Principles in the Age of Historicism*, New Haven and London 1991

K. W. Forster, 'L'ordine dorico come diapason dell'architettura moderna' in S. Settis (ed.), *I Greci. Storia arte cultura società*, vol. I, *Noi e i Greci*, Turin 1996, pp. 665ff

K. Solomonson, *The Chicago Tribune Tower Competition*, Cambridge 2000

J. Rykwert, 'L'architetto e la colonna. Il modello greco e la modernità' in S. Settis (ed.), *I Greci. Storia arte cultura società*, vol. III, *I Greci oltre la Grecia*, Turin 2001, pp. 1153ff

CHAPTER 6   THE 'CLASSICAL' IS NOT 'AUTHENTIC'

R. M. Rilke, *Auguste Rodin*, Leipzig 1919

P. Marconi, 'L'anticlassico nell'arte di Selinute' in *Dedalo*, XI, 1930, pp. 395–412

E. Buschor, *Vom Sinn der griechischen Standbilder*, Berlin 1942

U. Hausmann, *Die Apollosonette Rilkes und ihre plastischen Urbilder*, Berlin 1947

E. Langlotz, *Ancient Greek Sculpture of South Italy and Sicily*, New York 1965

W. Schnell, *Der Torso als Problem der modernen Kunst*, Berlin 1980

K. O. Blase, *Torso als Prinzip. Konzeption und Gestaltung*, Kassel 1982

M. Pratesi, 'Sulle tracce degli Etruschi. L'arte e la critica negli anni Venti e Trenta del Novecento', *Prospettiva*, no. 46, 1986, pp. 80ff

On Classic Ground: Picasso, Léger, De Chirico and the New Classicism 1910–1930, exhibition catalogue, London 1990

Das Fragment. Der Körper in Stücken, exhibition catalogue, Frankfurt 1990

S. Settis, 'Idea dell'arte greca d'occidente fra Otto e Novecento: Germania e Italia' in *Storia della Calabria*, vol. II, Rome and Reggio Calabria, 1994, pp. 855ff

G. W. Most, 'Polemos panton pater. Die Vorsokratiker in der Forschung der zwanziger Jahre' in H. Flashar (ed.), *Altertumswissenschaft in den 20er Jahren*, Stuttgart 1995, pp. 89–114

G. Boehm, U. Mosch and K. Schmidt (eds), *Canto d'amore. Classicism in Modern Art and Music, 1914–1935*, Basel 1996

G. Götte and J.-A. Bimie Danzker, *Rainer Maria Rilke und die bildende Kunst seiner Zeit*, Munich and New York 1996

G. W. Most, 'Vom Nutzen und Nachteil der Antike für das Leben. Zur modernen deutschen Selbstfindung anhand der alten Griechen', *Humanistische Bildung*, XIX, 1996, pp. 35ff

G. W. Most, 'Atene come scuola della Grecia' in S. Settis (ed.), *I Greci. Storia cultura arte civiltà*, vol. II/2, *Una storia greca: Definizione*, Turin 1997, pp. 1339ff

R. Wünsche, *Der Torso: Ruhm und Rätsel*, Munich 1998

A. Kostka and I. Wohlfarth (eds), *Nietzsche and 'an Architecture of our Minds'*, Los Angeles, Ca., 1999

G. W. Most, 'Die Entdeckung der Archaik. Von Ägina nach Naumburg' in B. Seidensticker and M. Vöhler (eds), *Urgeschichten der Moderne. Die Antike im 20. Jahrhundert*, Stuttgart and Weimar 2001, pp. 20ff

CHAPTER 7   GREEK 'CLASSICAL' VERSUS ROMAN 'CLASSICAL'

P. A. Paoli, *Rovine della città di Pesto*, Rome 1784

A. Riegl, *Spätrömische Kunstindustrie*, 1901, trans. and ed. Rolf Winke, Rome 1985

L. Cust and S. Colvin, *History of the Society of Dilettanti*, London 1914

J. von Schlosser, 'Die Wiener Schule der Kunstgeschichte. Rückblick auf ein Säkulum deutscher Gelehrtenarbeit in Österreich', *Mitteilungen des Österreichischen Instituts für Geschichtsforschung*, XIII, 1934, pp. 161ff

E. M. Butler, *The Tyranny of Greece over Germany*, Cambridge 1935

T. Hamlin, *Greek Revival Architecture in America*, New York 1944

M. L. Clarke, *Greek Studies in England, 1700–1830*, Cambridge 1945

R. Bianchi Bandinelli, 'Arte plebea' in *Dialoghi di archeologia*, I, 1967, pp. 7–19

D. Wiebenson, *Sources of Greek Revival Architecture*, London 1969

J. M. Crook, *The Greek Revival. Neo Classical Attitudes in British Architecture*, London 1972

G. Brunel (ed.), *Piranèse et les Français* (exhibition catalogue and conference papers), Rome 1976

J. Buxton, *The Grecian Taste. Literature in the Age of Neoclassicism, 1740–1820*, New York 1978

Berlin und die Antike, exhibition catalogue, Berlin 1979

R. Middleton and D. Watkin, *Neo-classical and 19th Century Architecture*, London 1980

J. Rykwert, *The First Moderns. The Architects of the Eighteenth Century*, Cambridge, Mass., and London, 1980

D. Crawford, 'Nature and Art. Some Dialectical Relationships', *Journal of Aesthetics and Art Criticism*, XLII, 1983, pp. 50ff

D. Constantine, *Early Greek Travellers and the Hellenic Ideal*, Cambridge 1984

L. Beschi, 'La scoperta dell'arte greca' in S. Settis (ed.), *Memoria dell'antico nell'arte italiana*, vol. III, Turin 1986, pp. 291ff

J. Raspi-Serra (ed.), *La fortuna di Paestum e la memoria moderna del dorico, 1750–1830*, Florence 1986

J. Traeger, *Der Weg nach Walhalla: Denkmallandschaft und Bildungsreise im 19. Jahrhundert*, Regensburg 1987

D. Watkin and T. Mellinghoff, *German Architecture and the Classical Ideal, 1740–1840*, London 1987

D. Stillmann, *English Neo-Classical Architecture*, London 1988

R. G. Kennedy and M. Bendtsen, *Greek Revival America*, New York 1989

S. Settis, 'Un'arte al plurale. L'impero romano, i Greci e i posteri' in E. Gabba and A. Schiavone (eds), *Storia di Roma, IV: Caratteri e morfologie*, Turin 1989, pp. 827ff

M. Iversen, *Alois Riegl: Art History and Theory*, Cambridge, Mass., 1993

M. Olin, *Forms of Representation in Alois Riegl's Theory of Art*, University Park, Penn., 1994

S. Anderson, *Peter Behrens and a New Architecture for the Twentieth Century*, Cambridge, Mass., 2000

J. Harris, *The Palladian Revival*, New Haven 1994

M. Warnke, 'Il bello e il naturale. Un incontro letale' in S. Settis, *I Greci. Storia arte cultura civiltà*, vol. I, *Noi e i Greci*, Turin 1996, pp. 343ff

R. Brilliant, 'Decadence and Decline' in *Grove Dictionary of Art*, VIII, 1996, pp. 595–7

L. Kantor Kazovsky, *Giovanni Battista Piranesi and the Aesthetical Problem of Roman Architecture*, dissertation, Jerusalem 1999

F. Salmon, *Building on Ruins. The Rediscovery of Rome and English Architecture*, London 2000

H. Hammer-Schenk, 'Leo von Klenzes Entwürfe für ein Denkmal des Weltfriedens. Eines Künstlers Traum (1814)' in *Ars et scriptura. Festschrift für Rudolf Preimersberger*, Berlin 2001, pp. 157ff

G. Piranesi, *Observations on the Letter of Monsieur Mariette. With opinions on architecture, and a preface to a new treatise on the introduction and progress of the fine arts in Europe in ancient times*, ed. J. Wilton-Ely, Los Angeles, Ca., 2002

S. Anderson, *Peter Behrens and a New Architecture for the Twentieth Century*, Cambridge, Mass., 2000

CHAPTER 8   THE 'CLASSICAL', LIBERTY AND REVOLUTION

B. Constant, *De la liberté des anciens comparée à celle des modernes*, Paris 1819

R. M. Rilke, 'Archaïscher Torso Apollos' in *Der neuen Gedichte anderer Teil*, 1908

M. Fontius, 'Winckelmann und die französische Aufklärung' in *Sitzungsberichte der deutschen Akademie der Wissenschaften zu Berlin*, Klasse für Sprachen, Literatur und Kunst, 1968, no. 1, pp. 3ff

H. M. Kallen, *Art and Freedom. A Historical and Bibliographical Interpretation of the Relations between the Ideas of Beauty, Use and Freedom in Western Civilization from the Greeks to the Present Day*, New York 1969

N. Himmelmann, *Utopische Vergangenheit. Archäologie und moderne Kultur*, Berlin 1976

T. W. Gaethgens (ed.), *Johan Joachim Winckelmann, 1717–1768*, Hamburg 1986

L. Uhling (ed.), *Griechenland als Ideal. Winckelmann und seine Rezeption in Deutschland*, Tübingen 1988

É. Pommier, 'Winckelmann et la vision de l'antiquité classique dans la France des Lumières et de la Révolution', *Revue de l'Art*, LXXXIII, 1989, pp. 9ff

É. Pommier (ed.), *Winckelmann. La naissance de l'histoire de l'art à l'époque des Lumières*, Paris 1991

H. Pfotenhauer, M. Bernauer and N. Miller (eds), *Frühklassizismus: Position und Opposition: Winckelmann, Mengs, Heinse*, Frankfurt 1995

A. Momigliano, *Pace e libertà nel mondo antico. Lezioni a Cambridge, gennaio-marzo 1940*, Florence 1996

C. Ampolo, *Storie greche. La formazione della moderna storiografia sugli antichi Greci*, Turin 1997, pp. 127–31

M. M. Sassi, 'La morte di Socrate' in S. Settis (ed.), *I Greci. Storia cultura arte civiltà*, vol. II. 2, *Una storia greca. Definizione*, Turin 1997, pp. 1323ff

É. Décultot, *Johann Joachim Winckelmann. Enquête sur la genèse de l'histoire de l'art*, Paris 2000

C. Avlami, 'Libertà liberale contro libertà antica. Francia e Inghilterra, 1752–1856' in S. Settis (ed.), *I Greci. Storia cultura arte civiltà*, vol. III, *I Greci oltre la Grecia*, Turin 2001, pp. 1311ff

É. Pommier, 'Arte e libertà: Winckelmann e i suoi seguaci' in S. Settis (ed.), *I Greci. Storia cultura arte civiltà*, vol. III, *I Greci oltre la Grecia*, Turin 2001, pp. 1287ff

É. Pommier, *Winckelmann, inventeur de l'histoire de l'art*, Paris 2003

J. J. Winckelmann, *Geschichte der Kunst des Alterthums*, 1974, trans II. F. Mallgrave and introduction by A. Potts, *History of the Art of Antiquity*, Los Angeles 2005

CHAPTER 9   THE 'CLASSICAL' AS A REPERTOIRE

M. Praz, *Gusto neoclassico*, Naples 2/1959

R. Rosenblum, *Transformations in Eighteenth-century Art*, Princeton, N.J., 1967

H. Honour, *Neoclassicism*, Harmondsworth 1968

M. Kemp, 'J.-L. David and the Prelude to a Moral Victory for Sparta', *Art Bulletin*, 1969, pp. 178ff

J. Starobinski, *1789. Les emblèmes de la raison*, Paris 1980

M. R. Levin, 'The Wedding of Art and Science in Late Eighteenth-century France. A Means of Building Social Solidarity' in *Eighteenth Century Life*, VII, 1982, no. 3 (May), pp. 54ff (art as 'moral technology')

H. Beck, P. C. Bol and E. Maek-Gérard (eds), *Ideal und Wirklichkeit der bildenden Kunst im späten 18. Jahrhundert*, Berlin 1984

A. Boime, *Art in an Age of Revolution, 1750–1800*, Chicago 1987

J. Onians, *Bearers of Meaning. The Classical Orders in Antiquity, the Middle Ages and the Renaissance*, New York 1988

J. Hargrove (ed.), *The French Academy: Classicism and its Antagonists*, Newark and London 1990

J. Lichtenstein, *The Eloquence of Color. Rhetoric and Painting in the French Classical Age*, Berkeley 1993

J.-C. Lebenstejn, *De l'imitation dans les beaux-arts*, Paris 1996

J. Rykwert, *The Dancing Column. On Order in Architecture*, Cambridge, Mass., and London 1996

D. G. Irwin, *Neoclassicism*, London 1997

G. Clarke and P. Crossley (eds), *Architecture and Language. Constructing Identity in European Architecture, 1000–1650*, Cambridge 2000

CHAPTER 10   THE REBIRTH OF ANTIQUITY

J. Michelet, *La Renaissance*, Paris 1855 (a collection of lectures given at the Collège de France in 1840; also published in vol. 7 of his *Histoire de France*, 17 vols, Paris 1833–1867)

J. Burckhardt, *Cultur der Renaissance in Italien*, Basel 1860

K. Borinski, 'Die Weltwiedergeburtsidee in den neueren Zeiten' in *Sitzungsberichte der Bayerischen Akademie der Wissenschaften*, 1919, I, pp. 1ff

C. Haskins, *The Renaissance of the Twelfth Century*, Cambridge, Mass., 1927

A. Warburg, *Die Erneuerung der heidnischen Antike*, Gesammelte Schriften, 2 vols, Leipzig 1932

A. von Salis, *Antike und Renaissance. Über Nachleben und Weiterwirken der Alten in der neueren Kunst*, Zürich 1947

W. K. Ferguson, *The Renaissance in Historical Thought. Five Centuries of Interpretation*, Cambridge, Mass., 1948

B. L. Ullman, 'Renaissance. The Word and the Underlying Concept', *Studies in Philology*, XLIX, 1952, pp. 105ff

K. H. Dannefeldt, *Renaissance. Medieval or Modern?*, Boston 1959

E. H. Gombrich, 'The Renaissance Conception of Artistic Progress and its Consequences' in *Norm and Form*, Oxford 1966, pp. 35ff

A. Buck, *Zu Begriff und Problem der Renaissance*, Darmstadt 1969

B. Bullen, 'The Source and Development of the Idea of the Renaissance in Early 19th Century French Criticism', *Modern Language Review*, LXXVI, 1981, pp. 311–22

F. Haskell and N. Penny, *Taste and the Antique. The Lure of Classical Sculpture 1500–1900*, New Haven and London 1982

B. Andreae and S. Settis (eds), *Colloquio sul reimpiego dei sarcofagi romani nel Medioevo*, Marburg 1983

W. Treadgold (ed.), *Renaissances before the Renaissance. Cultural Revivals of Late Antiquity and the Middle Ages*, Stanford, Ca., 1984

S. Settis (ed.), *Memoria dell'antico nell'arte italiana*, 3 vols, Turin 1984–6

N. Himmelmann, *Ideale Nacktheit*, Opladen 1985

S. Settis, G. Agosti and V. Farinella, 'Passione e gusto per l'antico nei pittori italiani del Quattrocento' in *Annali della Scuola Normale Superiore di Pisa*, series 3, XVII, 1987, pp. 1061ff

M. L. McLaughlin, 'Humanist Concepts of Renaissance and Middle Ages in the Tre and Quattrocento', *Renaissance Studies*, II, 1988, pp. 131ff

W. Kerrigan and G. Braden (eds), *The Idea of the Renaissance*, Baltimore 1989

N. Himmelmann, *Ideale Nacktheit in der griechischen Kunst*, Berlin and New York 1990

C. Landauer, 'Erwin Panofsky and the Renascence of the Renaissance', *Renaissance Quarterly*, XLVII, 1994, pp. 255–81

S. Settis, 'Ars moriendi. Cristo e Meleagro' in F. Caglioti (ed.), *Giornate di studio in ricordo di Giovanni Previtali. Annali della Scuola Normale Superiore di Pisa*, Quaderni, 9–10, series 4, Pisa 2000, pp. 145ff

CHAPTER 11   THE 'CLASSICAL' BEFORE 'CLASSICAL
ANTIQUITY'

Charles Perrault, *Parallèle des anciens et des modernes*, 1688–92

David Ruhnken, *Historia Critica Oratorum Greacorum*, Leyden
1768

R. Hinks, ' "Classical" and "Classicistic" in the Critics of Ancient Art'
in *Kritische Berichte zur kunstgeschichtlichen Literatur*, VI, 1937,
pp. 94ff

T. S. Eliot, *What is a Classic?*, London 1945

E. R. Curtius, *Europäische Literatur und Lateinisches Mittelalter*,
Bern 1948, trans. W. Trask, *European Literature and the Latin
Middle Ages*, Princeton 1973, pp. 276ff

A. Momigliano, 'Ancient History and the Antiquarian', *Journal of
the Warburg and Courtauld Institutes*, XIII, 1950, pp. 285ff
(also in *Contributo alla storia degli studi classici*, Rome 1955,
pp. 67ff)

H. Dieckmann and J. Seznec, 'The Horse of Marcus Aurelius',
Journal of the Warburg and Courtauld Institutes, XV, 1952,
pp. 198ff

W. Tatarkiewicz, 'Les quatre significations du mot *classique*', *Revue
internationale de philosophie*, XII, 1958, pp. 5ff

H. Baron, 'The Querelle of the Ancients and the Moderns as a
Problem for Present Renaissance Scholarship' in *Journal of the
History of Ideas*, XX, 1959, no. 1, pp. 3ff

L. Grassi, 'Nota intorno ai concetti di "antico" e "anticomoderno"
nella letteratura artistica' in *Scritti di storia dell'arte in onore di
Mario Salmi*, vol. III, Rome 1963, pp. 435–40

H. R. Jauss, introduction to the reprint (Munich 1964) of C. Perrault, *Parallèle des anciens et des modernes en ce qui regarde les arts
et les sciences*, Amsterdam 1693

H. Silvestre, '*Quanto iuniores, tanto perspicaciores*. Antécédents à la
Querelle des Anciens et des Modernes' in *Recueil commémoratif
du Xe anniversaire de la Faculté de Philosophie et Lettres de l'Uni-
versité Lovanium de Kinshasa*, Louvain and Paris 1968, pp. 231ff

E. Gössman, *Antiqui und Moderni im Mittelalter*, Munich, Pader-
born and Vienna 1974

A. Zimmermann (ed.), *Antiqui und Moderni. Traditionsbewusstsein
und Fortschrittsbewusstsein im späten Mittelalter*, Berlin 1974

C. Vasoli, 'La première Querelle des "anciens" et des "modernes"
aux origines de la Renaissance' in R. R. Bolgar (ed.), *Classical*

Influences on European Culture, AD *1500–1700*, Cambridge 1976, pp. 67–80

F. Fortini, 'Classico' in *Enciclopedia Einaudi*, vol. III, Turin 1978, pp. 192ff

T. Pelzel, *A. R. Mengs and Neoclassicism*, New York 1979

D. Buschunger and A. Crepin (eds), *La présentation de l'antiquité au Moyen Age*, Vienna 1982, pp. 49–66.

F. Kermode, *Classic. Literary Images of Permanence and Change*, Cambridge 1983

R. Hausherr, *Convenevolezza. Historische Angemessenheit in der Darstellung von Kostüm und Schauplatz seit der Spätantike bis ins 16. Jahrhundert*, Mainz 1984

S. Settis, 'Von auctoritas zu vetustas. Die antike Kunst in mittelalterlicher Sicht' in *Zeitschrift für Kunstgeschichte*, LI, 1988, pp. 157ff

A. Grafton, 'Germanograecia. Lo spazio del greco nel sistema d'istruzione' in S. Settis (ed.), *I Greci. Storia arte cultura società*, vol. III, *I Greci oltre la Grecia*, Turin 2001, pp. 1263ff

M. Bettini, *I quaderni del ramo d'oro*, IV, 2001, pp. 208ff (on the passage from Aulus Gellius)

M. Fumaroli, 'Les abeilles et les araignées' in *La Querelle des Anciens et des Modernes, XVIIe-XVIIIe siècles*, Paris 2001

Fabrizio Federici, unpublished research, 2005

CHAPTER 12   THE 'CLASSICISM' OF THE 'CLASSICAL' PERIOD

A. Körte, 'Der Begriff des klassischen in der Antike' in *Berichte d. Sächischen Akad. der Wissenschaften, Phil.-Hist. Klasse*, LXXXVI, 3, 1934

L. Edelstein, *The Idea of Progress in Classical Antiquity*, Baltimore 1967

P. Zanker, *Klassizistische Statuen. Studien zur Veränderung des Kunstgeschmäcks in der römischen Kaiserzeit*, Mainz 1974

R. Starn, 'Meaning Levels in the Theme of Historical Decline' in G. H. Nadel (ed.), *History and Theory. Studies in the Philosophy of History*, Middletown, Conn., 1975

P. Burke, 'Tradition and Experience. The Idea of Decline from Bruni to Gibbon' in *Daedalus*, no. 2, 1976, pp. 137–52

Le classicisme à Rome, Entretiens de la Fondation Hardt, no. 35, Geneva 1979

B. S. Ridgway, *Roman Copies of Greek Statues*, Ann Arbor 1984

M. J. Marek, 'Die Rezeption der antiken Kunstliteratur und ihre Voraussetzungen' in M. J. Marek, *Ekphrasis und Herrscheralle-gorie*, Worms 1985, pp. 1ff

J.-P. Niemeier, *Kopien und Nachahmungen im Hellenismus. Ein Beitrag zum Klassizismus des 2. und frühen 1. Jhs. v. Chr.* Bonn 1985

G. Bodei Giglioni, 'Dicearco e la riflessione sul passato', *Rivista Storica Italiana*, XCVIII, 1986, pp. 629–52

M. L. McLaughlin, 'Humanist Concepts of Renaissance and Middle Ages in the Tre- and Quattrocento' in *Renaissance Studies*, II, 1988, pp. 131–42

J. Griffin, 'Precious Stones', a review of *Imperial Spoils. The Curious Case of the Elgin Marbles* (1989) by Christopher Hitchens et al., *New York Review of Books*, XXXVI, 1989, no. 12, pp. 14–15

S. Settis, 'La trattatistica delle arti figurative' in G. Cambiano, L. Canfora and D. Lanza (eds), *Lo spazio letterario della Grecia antica*, vol. II, Rome 1993, pp. 469–98

S. Settis, 'Did the Ancients have an Antiquity? The Idea of Renaissance in the History of Classical Art' in A. Brown (ed.), *Language and Images of Renaissance Italy*, Oxford 1995, pp. 27–50

S. Settis, 'La conception de l'histoire de l'art chez les Grecs et son influence sur les théoriciens italiens du Quattrocento' in É. Pommier (ed.), *Histoire de l'histoire de l'art de l'Antiquité au XVIIIe siècle*, vol. I, Paris 1996, pp. 14ff

W. Ax, 'Dikaiarchs Bios Hellados und Varros de vita populi Romani' in *Rheinisches Museum*, CXLIII, 2000, pp. 337ff

CHAPTER 13   ETERNITY AMONGST THE RUINS

G. Rodenwaldt, 'Über das Problem der Renaissancen', *Archäolo-gischer Anzeiger*, 1931, pp. 318ff

G. Simmel, 'The Ruin' in K. H. Wolff (ed.), *Georg Simmel*, Columbus, Ohio, 1959, pp. 259ff

A. Momigliano, 'La caduta senza rumore di un impero' in *Sesto contributo alla storia degli studi classici*, Rome 1980, pp. 159–65

A. Kazhdan, 'Renaissance' in *The Oxford Dictionary of Byzantium*, vol. III, New York and Oxford 1981, pp. 1783ff

S. Settis, 'Continuità, distanza, conoscenza. Tre usi dell'antico' in S. Settis (ed.), *Memoria dell'antico nell'arte italiana*, vol. III,

Dalla tradizione all'archeologia, Turin 1986, 373–486 (including further bibliography)

A. Kazhdan, 'L'eredità antica a Bisanzio', *Studi Classici e Orientali*, XXXVIII, 1988, pp. 139–53, especially 144ff

F. Orlando, *Gli oggetti desueti nelle immagini della letteratura*, Turin 1993

E. de J. Douglas, 'Figures of Speech. Pictorial History in the Quinatzin Map of about 1542', *Art Bulletin*, LXXXV, 2003, pp. 281–309

W. Cupperi (ed.), *Senso delle rovine e riuso dell'antico*, Pisa 2004 (including F. M. Pontani, 'Ekleleimmena ereipia. I bizantini e le rovine antiche', pp. 45–54, on ruins in Byzantine culture)

S. Settis, 'Roma eternità delle rovine', *Eutropia*, no. 3, 2003, pp. 133–43 (including further bibliography)

Wu Hung, *Ruins in Chinese Visual Culture*, unpublished lecture, 1995

CHAPTER 14   IDENTITY AND OTHERNESS

The bibliography on Warburg is too vast to cover here. On his *Pathosformeln* see my 'Pathos und Ethos, Morphologie und Funktion' in J. Habermas and S. Settis, *Ernst Cassirer und die Bibliothek Warburg* (Vorträge aus dem Warburg-Haus, I), Berlin 1997, pp. 31–73; on *Mnemosyne*, see last Italian edition: A. Warburg, *Mnemosyne. L'atlante delle immagini*, ed. M. Ghelardi, Milan 2002. A general bibliography can be found in K. W. Forster and K. Mazzucco, *Introduzione ad Aby Warburg e all'Atlante della Memoria*, ed. M. Centanni, Milan 2002. For Warburg's travels amongst the Hopi, see S. Settis, 'Kunstgeschichte als vergleichende Kulturwissenschaft Aby Warburg, die Pueblo-Indianer und das Nachleben der Antike' in T. Gaehtgens (ed.), *Künstlerischer Austausch / Artistic Exchange. Akten des XXVIII Internationalen Kongresses für Kunstgeschichte, Berlin, 15–20. Juli 1992*, Berlin 1993, pp. 139–58; B. Cestelli-Guidi and N. Mann (eds), *Photographs at the Frontier. Aby Warburg in America, 1895–96'*, London 1998; and B. Cestelli-Guidi, 'La collection Pueblo d'Aby Warburg, 1895–96, in A. Warburg, *Le rituel du serpent. Récit d'un voyage en pays pueblo*, Paris 2003.

A version of Warburg's lecture on the snake ritual (1923) appears in the *Journal of the Warburg Institute*, series II, 1939, pp. 277–92. For Warburg's relationship with Usener, see A. Momigliano (ed.), *Aspetti di Hermann Usener filologo della religione*, Pisa 1982 (including M. M. Sassi, 'Dalla scienza delle religioni di Usener ad Aby Warburg', pp. 65–91). For the quotation from Burckhardt, see his 'Renaissance (Vorlesungen, Zürich 1856–57)' in M. Ghelardi, *La scoperta del Rinascimento. L'Età di Raffaello di Jacob Burckhardt*, Turin 1991, pp. 147ff.

CHAPTER 15   CYCLICAL HISTORIES

G. Charbonnier, *Entretiens avec Claude Lévi-Strauss*, Paris 1959, p. 38 (interview on French radio, including Lévi-Strauss's first mention of hot and cold societies)

F. Waters, *Book of the Hopi*, New York 1977

J. B. Jackson, *The Necessity for Ruins, and Other Topics*, Amherst, Mass., 1980

M. M. Sassi, 'Natura e storia in Platone', *Storia della Storiografia*, no. 9, 1986, pp. 104–28 (on catastrophes in the Greek world)

J. Assmann, *Das kulturelle Gedächtnis. Schrift, Erinnerung und politische Identität in frühen Hochkulturen*, Munich 1992

J. Carey, *The Irish National Origin-Legend: Synthetic Pseudohistory*, Cambridge 1994 (Quiggin Pamphlets on the Sources of Mediaeval Gaelic History, 1, published by the Department of Anglo-Saxon, Norse and Celtic, University of Cambridge)

C. Ginzburg, 'Oltre l'esotismo. Picasso e Warburg' in C. Ginzburg, *Rapporti di forza. Storia, retorica, prova*, Milan 2000, pp. 127–47

R. A. Nelson, *American Prophecy*, 2000, at *www.rexresearch.com/usa/usaproph.htm#us11*

J. Assmann, 'The Hot and the Cold in History' in *Measuring Historical Heat. Event, Performance and Impact in China and the West. Symposium in Honour of Rudolf G. Wagner on his 60th Birthday*, Heidelberg 2001, pp. 29–40; also at *www.sino.uniheidelberg.delconflsymposium2.pdf*

G. Cambiano, 'Catastrofi naturali e storia umana in Platone e Aristotele', *Rivista Storica Italiana*, CXIV, 2002, pp. 694–714

G. B. Conte, *Identità storica e confronto culturale. Dieci punti sulla tradizione umanistica europea*, unpublished

CHAPTER 16   THE FUTURE OF THE 'CLASSICAL'

For the works cited in this chapter, see: K. Marx, *Grundrisse*, 1857, Eng. trans., Harmondsworth 1973, pp. 110–11; C. Lévi-Strauss, 'Les trois humanismes' (1956) in *Anthropologie structurale deux*,

Paris 1973, pp. 319ff; J. Tainter, *The Collapse of Complex Societies*, Cambridge, 1988; and L. Morgan, 'Erasmus in Hanoi', *Times Literary Supplement*, no. 5250, 14 Nov 2003, p. 14.

The influence of Graeco-Roman art through Ghandara on Japanese art has been demonstrated by Katsumi Tanabe's articles in *Silk Road Art and Archaeology*, 8 vols, 1991–2002, and was recently highlighted by the exhibition *Alexander the Great. East-West Cultural Contacts from Greece to Japan* (exhibition catalogue, Tokyo and Osaka, 2003, including K. Tanabe, 'From Greece to Japan. The Aim and Significance of this Exhibition', pp. 19–23). For an excellent example of what comparative study of styles of thought can produce, see Geoffrey Lloyd, *Adversaries and Authorities. Investigations into Ancient Greek and Chinese Science*, Cambridge 1996.

Index